FOUR CENTURIES OF SCOTTISH WORSHIP

FOUR CENTURIES
OF
SCOTTISH WORSHIP

J. M. ROSS

THE SAINT ANDREW PRESS
EDINBURGH

© JOHN M. ROSS 1972

First published in 1972
by The Saint Andrew Press
121 George Street, Edinburgh

ISBN 0 7152 0185 9

The Picture on the Front Cover is from
an Illustration by A. S. Boyd, to an Edition of R. L. Stevenson's *A Lowden
Sabbath Morn*, published in 1907

Printed in Great Britain by
Alna Press Ltd., Broxburn & Edinburgh

Introduction

In 1960 I was invited by the Presbyterian Historical Society of England to deliver its thirty-third annual lecture. As the Church of Scotland was currently celebrating the four hundredth anniversary of the Scottish Reformation, I chose to speak on the changes which had taken place in the manner of public worship in Scotland during those four centuries. To keep a complicated subject within bounds I decided to give a description of how worship was actually conducted in the centennial years 1560, 1660, 1760, 1860, and 1960.

The lecture as delivered was published by the Society. The present booklet is a revision and expansion of the former work. In revising it I have not attempted to shift the picture forward by twelve years at each stage so as to make the final account completely contemporary, for the dates originally selected are more suitable for the purpose in hand. In 1560 the Scots Parliament had made the Mass illegal but the Church had not yet settled down to a pattern of Reformed worship; 1660 marks the closing year of the puritan revolution, before the modifications introduced under the restoration of episcopacy; by 1760 Scotland had reached about the middle point of stagnation between the violent religious controversies of the seventeenth and nineteenth centuries; in 1860 there was just beginning the modern movement for the reform of Scottish worship which has not yet spent its force; since 1960 the style of worship has not been entirely static and it may be no bad thing to put on record a typical service of twelve years ago.

How can one give a brief outline of the salient features in the chequered history of Scottish worship? It is not enough to select five centenary years and describe the state of worship in each, for most of the changes in Scottish worship have been gradual, beginning with the towns and spreading to the country from lowlands to highlands, so that at any point in history there might be one practice in Edinburgh, another in the Lowland countryside, and yet another in the Highlands, with perhaps further variants in the covenanting south-west or the episcopalian north-east. To simplify matters therefore, without undue distortion, let us invent a typical small town somewhere west of Edinburgh, south of Perth, and east of Glasgow, and let us give it the name of Kilmarkie. Nothing more definite may be said about its location except that it is at no great distance from Tannochbrae. If we describe what happens in Kilmarkie, we shall describe as nearly as possible what is happening in Scotland as a whole, without the necessity of mentioning also the numerous exceptions to the general practice; for Kilmarkie is never among the first to make a change, nor among the last to give up an old custom, nor has it any of the local peculiarities that are to be met with in the history of so many parishes.

CHAPTER ONE
1560

We begin, then, by finding ourselves in Kilmarkie on a Sunday morning in the autumn of 1560. Last August the Parliament made it a criminal offence to celebrate or attend mass, and we are interested to know what form of worship has taken its place.

At eight o'clock in the morning a bell rings to summon the town to worship: an early hour by later standards, but not so early as in the big towns. So we set off to the parish kirk carrying with us stools to sit on, for there are no pews in the church and we may not be early enough to hire a stool from the beadle. The old kirk, like most mediaeval churches, is a plain rectangle without transepts. It has a door at each end of the south side, rectangular windows in the south wall, pointed windows at the east and west ends, a bell hanging under the gable at the west end, and a thatched roof.

We enter the church and find the interior almost devoid of furnishings. The partition separating off the chancel at the east end has been removed in accordance with Matthew 27:51, and the altar, font, and all images (there were not many) have been taken out of the church and smashed up, as Gideon had destroyed the altar of Baal and the "grove" beside it (Judges 6:25–27). There are no pews, and the floor consists simply of bare earth (the usefulness of which will appear when we come to the arrangements for the Lord's Supper). The pulpit, however, remains in its former position in the middle of the south wall. Attached to the pulpit at ground level is a reading-desk or "lettron" (Scots for lectern).

A number of worshippers have already taken their places, the men on one side of the kirk, the women on the other. A few benches have been provided for the women to sit on, but

1

there is much competition for places, and as we enter the beadle is engaged in pacifying a "flyting" between two women. However, though manners are rough, most of the worshippers before sitting on their stools take off their hats and make a short prayer, either kneeling or standing.[1]

At half past eight a second bell is rung and the Reader enters. He is the former parish priest, but though he accepts the reformed faith he has had little education and is not considered competent to minister the word and sacraments. The Reader goes to the lettron and begins reading from his prayer-book:

> At what time soever a synner doeth repente hym of hys synne from the bottome of hys heart: I wyl put all his wickedness oute of my remembrance, sayth the Lorde.
> Dearely beloved brethren, the scripture moveth us in sundry places . . ."

and so on, for in Kilmarkie they use the English *Boke of Common Prayer* as revised in 1552;[2] indeed they have been using this for some years now, though they do not follow it with rigid exactness. They have heard that John Knox has brought with him a different prayer-book from Geneva, but they have not yet seen it, and it will be two years before the first Scottish Book of Common Order is printed, and some years more before its simpler ritual is adopted in Kilmarkie.

The morning service, as in England, consists of Morning Prayer, followed by the Litany, followed by the introductory part of the Communion Service, including the sermon but leaving out the Communion proper (which is only celebrated occasionally). During the prayers the men doff their caps and the women take their shawls off their heads. Instead of the psalms appointed in the prayer-book, the psalm sung today is the 91st, in the version appearing in the *Gude and Godlie Ballatis*,[3] for the selection in that book is all the parish knows. So we hear them sing—

> Quha on the hiest will depend,
> And in his secreit help will traist,
> Almychtie God sall him defend
> And gyde him with his haly Gaist . . .

—concluding with a doxology in the same metre. (Some neighbouring parishes are using the English metrical version of Sternhold and Hopkins; a Scottish Psalter, based on Sternhold and Hopkins, will not appear until 1562.)

The singing is unassisted by organ or any other musical instrument. This is not from any objection in principle to instrumental music in church—it has not yet been discovered in Kilmarkie that instruments in church are unchristian—but simply because the place is, and always has been, too poor to afford any such thing. The neighbouring church of Carpoch did have an organ, but it did not seem needed for reformed worship and was sold a few months ago, the proceeds being given to the poor.[4] Another neighbouring parish—Crocketbrig—having previously had a collegiate church, is fortunate in having four vicars-choral who are glad to serve the reformed liturgy; one sings the melody in the tenor, one sings a descant above, the other two sing in harmony below. They will not, however, be replaced, and in a few years' time the singing at Crocketbrig, like that in Kilmarkie, will be in plain unison unaccompanied.

3

The service continues. The Bible is read from the new Geneva version, a copy of which has just arrived. The Apostles' Creed (known in Scotland as the Belief) is sung from the version in the *Gude and Godlie Ballatis,* beginning:

We trow in God allanerlie . . .

This is a translation from Luther's version, and is sung to the appropriate German tune. The people respond "So be it" at the end of each prayer.

About ten o'clock the Minister enters. Kilmarkie is fortunate in having as its minister one of the Augustinian Canons from Inchbrendan Priory, who is of good education and understands the reformed doctrine; the neighbouring parishes of Carpoch, Crocketbrig, and Tulloweir have nothing better than a Reader, who conducts the entire service and in place of a sermon reads from the English Book of Homilies. The Minister goes up to the pulpit and kneels in silent prayer while the Reader continues to lead the service. Unlike the Reader, who wears no robes or vestments, the Minister conducts the service in the black scholar's cloak, bordered with fur, which he also wears out of doors.[5] This is considered appropriate as showing him to be a man of learning, without suggesting any associations with the Mass or other papistical corruptions. After the Reader has finished leading the people in the ten commandments, the Minister in his own words leads in prayer for the Queen, asking the Lord especially to turn her heart towards the reformed religion, and continues with a prayer that the congregation now present may be receptive to God's word. The Epistle, Gospel, and Nicene Creed are omitted as unnecessary, and the Minister proceeds to his sermon. The men replace their caps, but the women are not allowed to put up their shawls, as that would encourage slumber. During the sermon, which lasts about an hour, the beadle goes about the congregation, waking up sleepers.

After the sermon the offering is taken for the poor. As the people sit in no sort of order, this is no easy matter. The money is put in boxes on the end of poles, which elders push in and out among the people.[6]

This done, the Minister calls the people to pray for the whole estate of Christ's Church militant here in earth, and leads in a modified version of the form in the prayer-book. He then interrupts the prayer-book order by calling on the people to sing another psalm, as an act of praise to the Lord for his merciful deliverance of Scotland from the captivity of papistry, as a bird from the fowler's net. So the psalm chosen is the 124th—

> Except the Lord with vs had stand,
> Say furth, Israell, vnfenyeitlie . . .

At the conclusion of the psalm, the Minister reads one or two of the concluding collects from the prayer-book and gives the benediction. It is now about half past eleven, and the congregation disperses.

At half past one the congregation reassembles for the catechizing of children, after which the Reader conducts Evening Prayer according to the prayer-book. This is followed by a further sermon from the Minister, and the day's worship finishes about four o'clock or half past.

So much for the ordinary Sunday. In some of the bigger towns there are week-day services in the early morning, but Kilmarkie does not rise to that.

The Lord's Supper is administered irregularly once or twice a year. The Minister would like to have it once a month, as in Geneva, but his parishioners are not prepared for any violent departure from the tradition of receiving communion only once a year.[7] So we revisit Kilmarkie on the Communion Sunday in the autumn of 1560. On the previous Sunday there had been a meeting after morning worship at which all intending communicants had been asked to repeat the Lord's Prayer, the Belief, and the Ten Commandments; those who could do so were given tickets entitling them to communicate. (Metal tokens have not yet been introduced.) Tickets were not given to those known to be at variance with another parishioner: these were required to meet with the Minister

5

and Session the following day in order that all enmities might be reconciled before the community sat down in fellowship at the Lord's table.

On the communion day the first service begins at 5 a.m.; this is for the benefit of servants and others who have to work later. Special arrangements had to be made for elders and others to hold torches or candles to illuminate the church. The second service begins at 9 a.m. We enter the church for the second service, and are immediately struck by the fact that a long table, covered with white cloths, has been erected lengthwise along the kirk, with benches for sitting on either side of it; the table area has been fenced by a "travess" of stakes driven into the earth, with a gap at each end for one person to enter at a time.

The order of service follows generally that of the English prayer-book of 1552. After the usual preliminaries, including the hour-long sermon, the deacons[8] appointed for the purpose bring in the communion elements consisting of round unleavened shortbread cakes and claret wine mixed with water. The Minister then says Christ's "comfortable words" beginning—

Come unto me all that trauaille, and be heauye laden, and I shal refreshe you.

Thereupon the communicants give in their tickets to one of the two elders guarding the travess, and take their places on the benches at the side of the table. The Minister sits at the east end of the table. When all are seated, a basin in the shape of a quaich is passed round the table, and the communicants place in it their special offerings for the poor. After the consecration prayer, based on that in the prayer-book, the minister first receives both the bread and wine himself, and then passes a pewter basin of bread to those on each side of him; each takes a piece and passes the basin to the nearest communicant at the long table, who takes a piece and passes the basin on; when the basin has thus been passed to the foot of the table a deacon carries it back to the head of the table. The wine is

6

similarly passed round in two large pewter cups, from which each communicant drinks a good mouthful. (The basins and cups have been borrowed from the local tavern: the previous communion vessels, being associated with the idolatry of the Mass, and unsuitable for reformed worship,[9] have been sold and the proceeds placed in the poor's fund.) While the bread and wine are being passed round, the Minister reads the story of Christ's passion from one of the gospels.

When all have partaken, there is a second sitting of communicants at the table, and the same procedure is followed.[10] An attentive visitor would notice four variations from contemporary English practice: (1) Although the communion table is, as in England, placed lengthwise in the centre of the church, is is a much longer table (made of boards on trestles), and no one communicates unless actually sitting at it. (2) Though the communicants kneel for the prayers, they sit for the reception of the elements. (3) The elements were brought in during the service. (4) Before breaking the bread the Minister washes his hands in a "lavabo" bowl of water placed on the communion table, and dries them on a towel.

The communion is taken fasting both at the five o'clock and at the nine o'clock observance. The second service is brought to an end at one o'clock. Not all have been able to communicate, but there will be a further observance next Lord's Day for those unable for any reason to communicate this Sunday.

CHAPTER TWO
1660

Let us now suppose that we have gone to sleep like Rip Van Winkle, but for a hundred years, and that we wake up in Kilmarkie in the autumn of 1660. The changes that have taken place in church worship in that hundred years are simply staggering.

About 1570 Kilmarkie had adopted the Book of Common Order. The order of public worship in this book was much simpler than that of the English prayer-book, but it contained a few formal prayers which the Reader could use in the one-hour service before the Minister began his two-hour service from the pulpit. There were no longer any responses, but the people said "So be it" at the end of each prayer. In 1580 a "sang schule"[11] was instituted and singing in harmony reintroduced. In 1609 the separate office of Reader was allowed to lapse in Kilmarkie upon the retirement of the Reader appointed in 1574; from then on the Reader's functions were performed by the parish schoolmaster, who also held office as Session Clerk and Lettergae[12] or Uptaker of the Psalm (later known as Precentor). More and more liberties were being taken with the Book of Common Order when in 1637 Kilmarkie heard of King Charles's attempt to impose a new liturgy on Scotland. The reaction against this high-handed action swung Scotland over to sympathy with the new radicals, who sought to place public worship solely under the immediate prompting of the Holy Spirit and therefore to purge it of everything that could be regarded as carnal, formal, or idolatrous. We shall find many examples of such purgings having their effect on worship in Kilmarkie in 1660. Although for many years the General Assembly resisted all such innovations as strongly as it had rejected "Laud's Liturgy", eventually in 1643 it agreed, in effect, to grant local freedom, subject to the right of Presbyteries to exercise control.[13]

The new movement had become respectable because it had two strong forces on its side. First, its leaders appeared to be the more godly and spiritual element in the Church, for they did not need the support of forms in their worship; this must have created in many hearts a guilty feeling that a conservative adherence to the old ways was a sign of an inferior Christianity. Second, the new movement was dominant in Puritan England, and even those who did not care for the innovations were prepared to support their introduction in the interests of uniformity between the two kingdoms—albeit a very different kind of uniformity from that desired by King Charles and the bishops. (The new movement required an agreement to abstain from certain practices rather than a positive command to comply with new forms.)

In the middle of this controversy a new *Directory for the Publick Worship of God* had been drawn up by the Assembly of Divines at Westminster. In many respects this Directory represented a compromise between English Puritanism and Scottish traditional practice, but in some matters English influence had already ousted Scottish practice by the time the Directory was published, so that although it was approved and ordained by the General Assembly and Scots Parliament in 1645, it was not in most parts of Scotland closely complied with.

And now it is 1660, and Scotland is mightily pleased to have back again its covenanted King after ten years of Cromwell's soldiers. This is not going to make much difference to Scottish worship,[14] and as yet it has made none at all. But let us come down to Kilmarkie to see what is actually happening.

The first bell has rung at half past eight, and shortly afterwards we enter the kirk. The old building is not much changed in essentials, though we notice a number of minor differences. The thatch has been replaced by slate, and a little belfry has been built at the west gable, of bird-cage shape with a weather-vane on top. Inside, the pulpit is still in the middle of the south wall, but is a new and larger article installed in 1647 to replace the old pulpit which had become unsafe. A door has been made in the church wall to give direct access to the pulpit from outside and save the minister from having to pick his way among the stools of the congregation as he enters to conduct worship. The "lettron" below the pulpit is now large enough to provide seats for the elders, as well as for the Uptaker of the Psalm in the middle. The new pulpit is also furnished with an hour-glass, and a bracket to hold the baptismal basin. On the wall on either side of the pulpit are painted the Lord's Prayer and Ten Commandments. Near the pulpit is the pillory or stool of repentance—a contraption like an enormous pair of steps, which will come into use later this morning. Opposite the pulpit are several finely carved box pews belonging to the

lairds and one or two well-to-do merchants; the rest of the
congregation still sit on forms or stools or on the earthen
floor. From the roof hang two brass chandeliers to light the
kirk on dark winter days; the box pews have their own candle-
sticks of turned wood.[15]

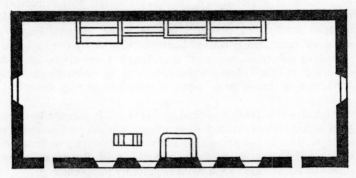

As we enter we are asked for our offerings by an elder, who
stands at the door by a small table on which is a box or "brod"
containing an assortment of small coins. The General Assembly
in 1573 had prohibited the taking of collections otherwise than
at the kirk doors; decisions of Assembly have not always been
carried out in Kilmarkie, but the taking of the collection
during service had been found inconvenient about that time
and abandoned.

We go inside and find the men and women still sitting
separately—except of course in the lairds' pews. The worshippers no longer stand or kneel for private prayer before taking
their seats; to kneel or "bow" for prayer at any time in church
is now held to imply that the part of the church towards which
one bows is more sacred than the rest of the building: that
would be papistical idolatry and must not be countenanced.
Hence the new Directory requires the worshippers to take their
places "without adoration, or bowing themselves towards one
place or another." Even standing for prayer might be open to
the same objection, and so the people sit for prayer throughout
the service.[16]

There is now no Reader's service, because Scripture does not recognise the office of Reader (though that office has recently been restored in Carpoch). Worship begins at nine o'clock with a second bell and the entry of the Minister into the pulpit. He wears a black gown and bands. Naturally he no longer "bows in the pulpit" (i.e. kneels for private prayer) before commencing the service; yet he does bow *from* the pulpit—not to God, but to the chief laird (or "heritor"), George Craik of Dowie, who returns the compliment. After this preliminary, the Minister announces that the following Thursday has been appointed by the Presbytery as a special day of fasting and humiliation, in order that the people may take occasion of the poor harvest and the recent attack of plague to abase themselves before God, confess the crying sins of themselves and the nation, and pray that the new King and the Parliament may take order for the better honouring of God's laws in the future. To this end the parish is required to attend a special service in the kirk that day at nine hours in the forenoon.[17]

The Minister then calls upon the congregation to worship God and leads them in a short introductory prayer. The men still take off their hats or bonnets for the prayers, but no longer add "So be it" at the end. Then follows a psalm. We are lucky to have any singing at all, for in the Kirk of Kilmarkie psalm-singing was restored only a few years ago after its discontinuance in 1648; there is still no singing in Tulloweir. The psalm is now sung in a most astonishing manner: the Uptaker intones the first line in a kind of recitative on the first note of the tune, then sings the line over to the proper notes of the tune, the congregation singing with him; the same process is repeated for each line to the end of the psalm. This method of "lining out" the psalm was introduced from England, where few people could read, but soon took a firm hold on Scotland, where illiteracy was not as rare as some would like to believe. The words of the psalm are from the new Scottish Psalter of 1646 (the same version as is still in use today); the singing is still without instrumental accompaniment, and no attempt is made to sing in harmony, the "sang

11

B

schule" having gone out of existence a long time ago. The congregation remain seated while they sing—and well they may, for a complete psalm, lined out and sung with due reverence, could easily last for twenty minutes. No doxology is now sung at the end of the psalm; this is one of the "nocent ceremonies" objected to by the puritans as formal and therefore popish and unspiritual.

By this time the beadle will have locked the kirk doors to prevent the ungodly from slipping away before the end of the service.

After the psalm the Minister reads a few verses of Scripture and then delivers a half-hour lecture expounding them. This is not quite what the Directory intended: it is there contemplated that normally a chapter at least will be read from each Testament, and that expositions will be brief and exceptional; but English Puritan taste considers the bare reading of Scripture formal and unedifying, and the fashion of lecturing instead has become widespread in Scotland.

The lecture is followed by a prayer lasting some fifteen minutes; it consists of a heartfelt confession of sins and a request for illumination from the preaching of the Word. After this the men cover their heads again as before, and settle down to the sermon, which this morning lasts only an hour and a quarter; the hour-glass gives the Minister some idea of when to stop, but sometimes when he feels the Spirit on him he may preach for up to two hours. The text of today's sermon is an "ordinarie", that is to say a text on which a series of sermons is preached; the present series is on Jeremiah 31:31, "I will make a new covenant with the house of Israel", and today's sermon is on the fifth of the eight respects in which the old covenant was imperfect.

After the sermon comes what some of the more carnal among the congregation will consider the most interesting part of the morning's proceedings—the rebuking of offenders. Perched upon the pillory in various positions according to the gravity of their offences, and clothed in sackcloth, sit several offenders against the godly discipline of the kirk, and each in turn receives his admonition from the Minister. First, a final

12

rebuke and solemn absolution for James Thomson, appearing for the thirty-ninth time for a trilapse in adultery, but now adjudged by the Session to have given undeniable evidence of true repentance;[18] then a serious word for Elspat Wemyss, appearing for the fifth time for fornication; then to Robert Hay for the third time for selling short weight; and finally to Margaret Galloway for the first and only time for tale-bearing.[19]

After this interlude the Minister begins his long prayer of thanksgiving and intercession, which lasts about half an hour. The Lord's Prayer is no longer used anywhere in the service, for it is a form of words, and all forms impede the Spirit.[20] The "Belief" has also, of course, been discontinued, because it is not only a form, but a merely human composition.[21]

This prayer is followed by a second psalm, sung as before, after which the Minister gives the benediction. Immediately the congregation rises without further devotion and disperses. The service has lasted well over three hours.

After the service there is a short interval for lunch. This is followed by the catechizing of children, and then the bell rings for the afternoon service. This contains neither lecture nor rebuking of penitents and is accordingly much shorter, lasting a mere two hours.

The observance of the Lord's Supper has greatly changed from a hundred years ago; it is a less frequent but a more solemn occasion. In theory it takes place annually, but many parishes do not come up to that standard, and in Kilmarkie there was no observance between 1654 and 1660 because of the bitter feeling between the Resolutioners and Protesters. The 1660 communion in Kilmarkie begins[22] with a service of preparation on the Saturday. (In Tulloweir they go one better and begin with the Thursday fast day which was soon to become universal in Scotland.)

On Sunday there is only the one service, which begins about 8 a.m. There is no longer any obligation to communicate fasting, and the service lasts many hours. The table, as before, runs the length of the kirk, but now there has been added at the east end a small cross table for the officiating ministers.

13

As before, the table area is guarded by a "travess" of stakes with an entrance at each end. After conducting morning worship as usual from the pulpit the Minister comes down and stands at the middle of the cross table; on either side of him stand the Ministers of Carpoch and St. Ringan's who have come to assist him, as a "communion season" is now more than one minister can get through unaided.

While the ministers are going to the table, two elders bring in the bread and wine from a temporary store outside the kirk. The bread consists of ordinary white bread cut into long slices and placed in two large basins; the wine is claret unmixed with water, and has been poured into the wide silver mazer provided by the heritors in 1617. Two other elders stand guard at the entrances to the table to ensure that no unworthy person is admitted. The parish has been well catechized beforehand by the Minister and elders, and tokens issued to all judged fit to communicate; but the mere presentation of a token does not necessarily secure admission to the table, for the elders have a list of those who are not to be admitted in any case, e.g. because they do not practise family worship.[23] The congregation, according to the new fashion, is swollen by visitors from some neighbouring parishes where there is no communion this year; these bring with them testimonials from their ministers. Not all, however, who have tokens or testimonials will dare to sit down at the table, for it has been solemnly "fenced"— that is to say the Minister, while inviting all who are penitent to communicate, has delivered a stern warning to the impenitent, the unforgiving, and the hardened sinners not to eat and drink damnation to themselves (1 Cor. 11:29) by communicating at the Lord's table. Even so, there are far too many communicants for all to sit at one table, so the communicants are served in relays, a separate communion service being held for each successive "table". Indeed there is not room in the kirk for all who wish to attend (whether as communicants or spectators), so a good number have to wait outside. From time to time these are addressed by one of the ministers, who preaches to them from a "tent". (This was not what we now know as a tent, but was a wooden hut something like a sentry-box, with a tent-like roof; the object was to give the preacher shelter from wind and rain, but it was subsequently discovered that if properly used the "tent" acted as a very effective sounding-board and enabled the speaker to address a vast crowd.[24]) Not everyone, however, listens to these edifying discourses; some occupy themselves in less godly pursuits, and may even be too much the worse for liquor to be fit to partake of the Sacrament. Already we meet the beginnings of the extraordinary communion gatherings of a hundred years later.

The service at the table follows the new Directory, but is not greatly different from that in the Book of Common Order which had been used in Kilmarkie from 1570 to 1650. It begins with an exhortation, then there follows the reading of the words of institution (1 Cor. 11:23–26), after that the prayer of thanksgiving and sanctification of the elements, then the distribution. For this purpose the Minister takes a piece of bread and hands it to the minister on his right, and another to the minister on his left, saying "Take ye, eat ye, this is the body of Christ which is broken for you; do this in remembrance of him." Each of these breaks off a morsel to eat and hands the bread on to the nearest communicant at the table.[25] Elders carry the basins round to provide fresh pieces of bread when the original pieces have been consumed. When all have partaken of the bread the Minister takes the cup and gives it to the minister on his right saying "This cup is the new testament in the blood of Christ, which is shed for the remission of the sins of many; drink ye all of it." The one cup is passed right round the table, each taking a little sip from it. The Minister does not communicate because he will be served by a brother minister who will conduct the service at the next sitting. Nothing is now read during the distribution of the bread and wine: this takes place in silence in accordance with the Act of Assembly of 7 February 1645. When all have received, the Minister gives a short exhortation and a final prayer of thanksgiving. No collection is now taken at the table—this has been forbidden by Act of Assembly in 1648.

15

The communicants now leave, and while the table is dissolving and re-filling a portion of a psalm is sung (as enjoined by the Assembly in 1645), and elders bring in any necessary fresh supplies of bread and wine. When the last table has been served, the Minister gives a concluding address to the whole congregation, and after prayer and a psalm of thanksgiving the congregation disperses at about 2 p.m. But this is not all. On the following day (which is observed like a Sabbath) the people reassemble for a two-hour thanksgiving service in the afternoon, including a sermon of an hour's duration from the Minister of St. Ringan's; this sermon, known as "the close of the work", is a summary of all the addresses and sermons of the week-end. There is, however, no further observance of the Sacrament next Sunday; those who could not communicate this year must wait a few years for the next observance, or else make their way to the celebration in some other parish, armed with a testimonial from their Minister.

CHAPTER THREE
1760

Another hundred years have passed, eventful enough in the national life and ecclesiastical politics, but not productive of great alterations in worship. The change to episcopal government in 1662 made little difference to parish life, and in Kilmarkie the only effect on worship was that the minister recited the Lord's Prayer at the end of his prayer before sermon, a doxology was sung at the end of each psalm, and the lecture was replaced by the reading of a chapter or two of Scripture.[26] All these changes were reversed at the Revolution in 1689 because they were associated with prelacy, and the mid-17th-century innovations became firmly entrenched as the national mode of worship.[27] We shall not therefore find any fundamental differences in Kilmarkie in

1760, but even in static 18th-century Scotland time does not stand still, and a number of changes have occurred, which will be duly noted.

One of the changes impinges on our notice at the outset of the day: the hour of morning worship is again a little later, and the first bell does not ring until ten o'clock. We set out for the old kirk, and find it considerably altered. After putting our money in the large basin standing at the door, we enter the church and find that the floor is now tiled and completely filled with pews, except for a space along the centre to take the long table on communion days, and a corner at the west end where there are some benches for those who are too poor to afford a pew. (The fact that standards of comfort in church vary according to social position does not strike anyone in 1760 as unchristian or unnatural.) The pews are painted green and fitted with doors. The provision of pews meant that there was no longer enough room for all the congregation on the ground level of the old building, and to accommodate the growing population two expedients have been resorted to: an extension of the church has been built in the middle of the north side, so that the building is now T-shaped; and galleries or "lofts" have been erected on all except the south wall. The pillory is still there, but is no longer used, offenders now being rebuked in private before the Session. The chief heritor, Lord Plenish of Auchterniddrie, has a heated retiring room behind his pew in the north loft, which is reached by a turnpike stair; here he and his family partake of a cold "collation" between the services. Most of the other heritors have their pews in the north loft in the original building; some of these are decorated with funeral escutcheons.

The congregation is now assembling, and we notice that the men and the women no longer sit separately, but each family sits together in its pew. The worshippers do not, of course, make any act of devotion on taking their seats; nor do the men take off their hats or bonnets.

At half past ten the bell is rung again, and the Precentor (to give him his new title), wearing a black gown, stands up in the "lettron" to give out the opening psalm. Before he does

17

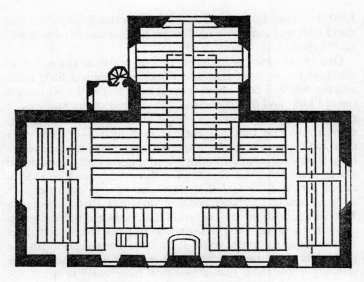

Dotted lines indicate lofts

this, however, there is an "intimation" to be made. By authority of the Session he reads out a "brief" which has been sent to all parishes in England and Scotland by command of the King, appealing for contributions for the erection at Saarbruch (Saarbrücken) of a church, a minister's house and school for the use of distressed Reformed Protestants from Catholic states who had been granted leave to settle at Saarbruch in order to enjoy the free exercise of their religion; there will be a collection for this purpose at the doors at the end of the service.[28] After this intimation the Precentor announces what is known as the "gathering psalm" (because it is sung while the people are still gathering for worship). This way of beginning the service in advance of the Minister's entry was not contemplated by the Directory for Public Worship, but has become widespread by 1760; it is a vestigial relic of the old Reader's Service, which in some parishes was never abandoned in spite of the puritan revolution, and in others was reintroduced during the episcopate of 1662–89.[29] However, in Kilmarkie no one associates this with prelacy, and the service proceeds.[30]

The psalm is still "lined out" in the manner described above, and no attempt is yet made to sing in harmony. The psalm creeps along its slow course until about 10.45, when the minister enters the pulpit, wearing a blue gown. (His colleagues in the neighbouring parishes wear ordinary clothes and a hat, and no gown.) On taking his place in the pulpit he bows to all the heritors in careful order of precedence, first to Lord Plenish, then to Sir James Craik of Dowie, then to Hugh Inglis of Benchlieknowes, and finally to William Gray of Madder. Each laird returns the bow to the Minister. The Minister then leans forward and taps the Precentor on his head with his psalm-book, as a signal to him that it is time the singing came to an end; the Precentor finishes the verse and sits down. (The congregation have of course been sitting throughout the singing.)

The Minister now leads in the first prayer, which lasts about a quarter of an hour. During the prayer the men uncover their heads and the congregation no longer sits but stands. The prayer is followed by the lecture, which as before takes the place of the reading of Scripture and lasts about half an hour. For the last year the minister has been working steadily through the Epistle to the Hebrews and today's lecture is on chapter 10, verses 23 to 28. After the lecture, had we been in Crocketbrig or Carpoch, we would have joined in another psalm, but at Kilmarkie the service goes straight on to the five-minute prayer for illumination, after which the Minister begins his sermon. Only the older men replace their bonnets for the sermon; the custom is slowly dying out. The sermon is still delivered from memory, for the reading of sermons is strongly objected to: after all, what does a young man go to college for, if not to learn to speak without notes?[31] The sermon is no longer preached on an "ordinary". Today's is on the text "The fear of the Lord is the beginning of wisdom" (Proverbs 9:10), which is handled under seven heads: 1. Who the Lord is; 2. The nature of godly fear; 3. Why the Lord is to be feared; 4. What wisdom is; 5. The necessity of wisdom; 6. How godly fear induces wisdom; 7. An appeal to all present to be wise in time. The sermon lasts only an hour; those who want a longer sermon must go to Tulloweir or join the Seceders. After the sermon there follows the usual long prayer of thanksgiving and intercession, during which the congregation again stands; this lasts only twenty minutes—perhaps because this is quite long enough for people to endure the strain of standing. At the conclusion of this prayer the people sit down for a second psalm. (A book of Paraphrases of other passages of Sacred Scripture was published in 1745 and has been approved by the General Assembly, but no one in Kilmarkie would dream of singing them even if he had heard of them.) The psalm lasts about ten minutes and then the congregation is dismissed about one o'clock with a benediction. The service is distinctly shorter than in 1660; it has lasted only two and a half hours.

The congregation is dismissed; but many of them stay behind in their pews to eat some lunch, for the afternoon service will soon begin. During this interval, for the edification of those who stay behind, two boys from Kilmarkie Academy answer questions from the Shorter Catechism.

The afternoon service begins at two o'clock. It differs little from that of 1660, consists mostly of sermon, and lasts less than two hours. There is no second service in Tulloweir or Crocketbrig.

The Lord's Supper[32] is observed in Kilmarkie once every two or three years; the people cannot afford it oftener, because of the great expense of giving hospitality to the multitude of visitors. The 1760 "occasion" takes place in July at the time of full moon. It is a bigger event than in 1660: thousands flock in not only from Crocketbrig, Carpoch, and Tulloweir, but also farther afield from parishes such as Traive, Gaskethill, Braegunnion, St. Ringan's, and Kirkton of Glenderris. Six ministers come to help for some or all of the time; those who are present on Sunday leave their churches closed, for most of their parishioners are in Kilmarkie too.

The "occasion" is a secular as well as a religious event, having much in common with the annual fairs held in a number of places, at which employees are hired, lovers make assignations, and travelling salesmen and entertainers ply their trade. Servants and labourers, as part of their conditions of service, are regularly given time off to attend, say, "one occasion and two fairs" in the course of the year. The only difference between an ordinary fair and an "occasion" (or "holy fair") was that at the latter a solemn celebration of the Sacrament was combined with the devotions paid to Bacchus, Venus, and Mammon. The "communion season" opens on the Thursday, which is observed as a "fast day", which means in practice that it is treated as a "sabbath" like any Sunday; none but absolutely essential work is done, and all recreation is prohibited. Whether there was also abstinence from food is not clear. The day, however, is not observed merely negatively: down by Fethy Water on Kilmarkie Green there has been placed the "tent", and from this a continuous series of addresses is given throughout the day to attentive crowds by a succession of ministers. Friday is a normal working day again. (In the highlands it is the great day of the Men's Meeting, when "the men", that is the spiritual giants among the laity, "speak to the Question" that has been put down for discussion; but the Kilmarkie elders are not of that stature.) On Saturday there is more tent-preaching, culminating in a great "preparation sermon", after which tokens are distributed according to lists kept by the elders. By now most of the visitors have arrived, and all about among the trees and bushes can be seen people busily reading their bibles or engaging in earnest prayer. Others indulge in less godly pursuits. Some never stray far from the ale-house; young men and women wearing their best finery walk about for mutual admiration; and among them all hawkers, sturdy beggars, and gangs of travelling tinkers are eagerly at work. The inextricable mixture of holy and profane is thus described by Burns:

> Here, some are thinkin' on their sins,
> An' some upo' their claes;
> Ane curses feet that fyl'd his shins,
> Anither sighs an prays.

The same duality is thus described by Burnet:[33] "In the tragi-comic welter of weeping, mocking, squeezing, cursing, lecherous humanity, many of them with no tokens, it was impossible to be sure where genuine piety lay". Nevertheless "many devout and simple saints found in these Communions, despite their uncouth and often irreverent setting, a true and intensely joyful trysting time with their Saviour at his Table."

The Sunday services, known as the Great Work, begin at an early hour and continue until dusk with a separate "action sermon" for each successive table, preached by different ministers in turn. The procedure in church is similar to that of a hundred years before. The long table is set up in the space in the middle of the church, fenced round with a per-manent wooden partition in which there is a gate at each end. There is no room for a cross table at the end, and the offici-ating minister simply stands at the east end of the long table. The table is rather shorter than it was before the pews were installed; consequently more services are necessary to enable all to comunicate who wish to do so, especially as the number of visitors is so much greater, and not by any means all are deterred by the "fencing of the table": the result is that the proceedings take much longer than in 1660 and occupy the whole of a summer's day. The old communion cup and basins are no longer in use: they were stolen in 1745 by the rebel army to raise badly needed money; the heritors have not felt able yet to replace them, especially as the need only arises every second or third year; consequently communion vessels have had to be borrowed for this occasion from Carpoch. The cup, of more recent design, is taller and narrower than the old mazer. Not all the ministers conduct the service in quite the same way: some of them let the bread and wine go round in silence, others deliver an additional discourse during the distribution.[34] At the end of each service, before the comuni-cants rise, a sort of quaich is passed round the table in which the communicants place special offerings for the poor. (In other places, such as Crocketbrig and Tulloweir, this extra collection is taken at the doors as the communicants leave the kirk.) There is of course no need to stay in the kirk after communicating, and indeed communicants are encouraged to leave, in order to make way for others of the vast throng which the building is far too small to accommodate. But those who go out of doors need have no lack of spiritual sustenance: there is a continuous supply of addresses on Kilmarkie Green for those who have come out of church or have not yet been able to get in.

The festival continues, as before, on the Monday. There are further tent-preachings on Kilmarkie Green, and eventually in the afternoon the Minister of Gaskethill "closes the Work"; he has been chosen for this because he has a good memory and a powerful voice, and knows how to make the most of the "tent" as a sounding box. To a vast, hushed, and deeply moved audience he summarizes all the addresses delivered during the "occasion", and leaves his listeners with a few joyful but serious thoughts to keep in mind for another year until the Tulloweir sacrament in the following June. Then the atmosphere relaxes. Friends and relatives will soon have to separate again, so the rest of the day is spent in social parties, the chief of which is a sumptuous dinner at the Manse for the officiating ministers, who are worn out physically and emotion-ally with their exertions; a few others are specially invited to join this party, at which the unconsumed sacrament wine is finished off. Everyone in his own way finishes the day in convivial mood, and then the visitors walk back the ten, twenty, or thirty miles to their homes. Of these, to quote Burns again:

> There's some are fou' o' love divine;
> There's some are fou' o' brandy.

Before we finish with 1760 it should be mentioned that Kilmarkie now has a small Episcopal congregation which meets illegally in a building that looks like two private houses with separate doors, but is so arranged internally that listeners in various parts of both houses can at least hear the service. The worship follows the English Book of Common Prayer. There is also a small body of Seceders, whose worship differs from that in the Church of Scotland only by being a little more conservative. The sermon is more Calvinistic and less ethical, and each item in the service tends to take a little longer, so that the whole lasts three hours or more.[35]

CHAPTER FOUR
1860

We now go to sleep for another hundred years and revisit Kilmarkie in 1860. Externally, there has been a considerable change. The old kirk, long in a very poor state of repair, was finally pulled down and rebuilt in 1823, the fourth Lord Plenish having become wealthy in the recent war from the discovery of iron on the Auchterniddrie estate. The new building is on the site of the old, but rather wider from north to south. It has a tower at the west end, with an embattled parapet and pinnacles at the corners, and the windows are of the Gothic shape now becoming fashionable; the building is not, however, an elaborate imitation of mediaeval models, like many churches of the later nineteenth century: parsimony and good taste combined to keep the architecture within the simplicity of "Heritors' Gothic". We enter by the west door and find that the old seventeenth-century pulpit has been erected at the east end and graced by a curving double stair. Originally the Minister entered the church by a small door at the foot of one of the stairs, but recently a vestry has been added outside, from which he enters through this door. The body of the kirk is filled with pews all facing the pulpit and separated by a central passage broad enough to contain the long table placed there on sacrament days. There is as yet no permanent table, no font, no organ. A gallery, reached by stairs in the tower, runs round the south, west, and north walls.

The general pattern of Sabbath worship (for the Lord's Day is now commonly known as "the Sabbath") is the same as that of a century before, but a number of changes have

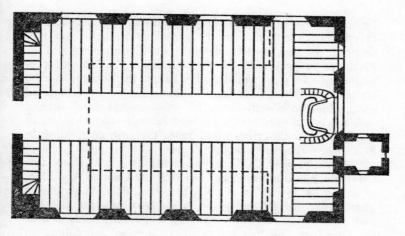

Dotted lines indicate gallery

taken place, and special attention will be paid to these.[36] A liturgical revolution began in Scotland in the eighteen-sixties, but some preliminary tremors had already had their effect on Kilmarkie.

The warning bell now rings at half past ten for an eleven o'clock service.[37] We put our money in the collection plate at the door and take our places. We notice that although the men still enter the church covered, they take off their hats or caps on entering their pews, but the worshippers still perform no other act of devotion before the service begins. There is no "gathering psalm" before the entry of the Minister. The service begins with the Beadle coming out of the vestry and carrying the bible and psalm-book into the pulpit. Immediately he has come down the steps the Minister goes up to the pulpit and the Beadle shuts the door behind him. The Minister is wearing a black gown and bands and black gloves, but no academic hood (although he is in fact an M.A. of St. Andrews). He does not bow to any lairds: indeed only the Madder family now attend the parish kirk, the other lairds having joined the

Episcopalians—not because they are convinced of the necessity of episcopacy but because the gentry prefer the order and decorum of episcopalian worship to the uncouth riot of Presbyterian prayers.[38] There is, however, a different preliminary to be got through today before the worship can be started on its course: the Precentor (wearing the rather tattered gown which he inherited from his predecessors) stands up and calls the banns of marriage between James Stirling residing in Auchterend in this parish and Janet Livingstone residing in Pitcaddie in the parish of Carpoch.[39]

"Let us worship God," says the Minister, and announces the opening psalm. (As recently as 1856 the General Assembly, repeating its injunction of 1705, urged ministers to pay more attention to the Directory for Public Worship, but this has had no effect so far as the opening of worship is concerned; the Directory says that the minister, after solemn calling on the congregation to the worshipping of the great name of God, is to begin with prayer, and does not mention psalm-singing till just before the benediction, but Kilmarkie, like the rest of Scotland, is convinced that a psalm is the proper way to begin worship.) The Minister reads out as much of the psalm as is to be sung, and the Precentor then leads the singing. His method of doing so, not quite the same as that of a hundred years before, would be accurately described in the following lines:

> What unction in the varied tones
> As aff the line he screeds us,
> Syne bites the fork, an' bums the note,
> Ere to the tune he leads us[40].

That is to say, he no longer intones the line but reads it in a speaking voice. (In Tulloweir the line is still chanted in the traditional manner, but in Carpoch the psalm is lined out only "between tables" at the communion, and in Crocketbrig lining-out has been abandoned altogether.) The precentor is now assisted by a choir (or "band", as it is called), which sits in the west gallery. Another innovation is the tuning-fork with which he pitches the note, but this is the only instrument of music in use. Some innovators are trying to introduce organs into churches in Glasgow and Edinburgh, but for the present Kilmarkie is solidly and firmly opposed to such an engine of ritualism.[41]

After the psalm, which is still sung sitting, there comes a long prayer as before, for which the congregation still stands—at least for the first few minutes, but by the end of the prayer many are slouching over the pew-backs and the infirm have resumed their seats. The prayer is still couched in rather esoteric language, with profuse allusions to what would now be regarded as the less important parts of Scripture; one such allusion reminds the Minister of another, and the prayer rambles on for a quarter of an hour or more until the Minister feels it is time to stop, whereupon he concludes with another innovation—the recitation of the Lord's Prayer. Of course the congregation do not join in; that would be ritualism; but they tolerate his use of it in the pulpit, though it is not yet in use in any of the neighbouring parishes.

This prayer is followed not by a lecture, but by the plain reading of a chapter from the Bible. The lecture has only recently been given up in Kilmarkie; it is still delivered in Tulloweir and Gaskethill, with only a brief reading from Scripture, but in the latter parish, as in many others, there is no sermon in addition to the lecture. After the reading of Scripture comes another novelty—the singing of a second psalm. Then after the usual short prayer for illumination the Minister delivers his sermon, which he reads from a manuscript, but surreptitiously, for many of his parishioners still seem to think that the Holy Spirit can give a preacher his words only in the pulpit, not in the study[42]. As the sermon has absorbed the lecture it contains a good deal of exposition of the scripture passage previously read. There is no hour-glass and the sermon lasts only 45 minutes. After the sermon there follows the intercessory prayer, still nearly twenty minutes in length, and at the end of this is the proper place for the Minister's "intimations". Today the announcement is that on Wednesday and Thursday he will visit and catechize families residing in Patrick's Wynd, Wellington Street, and Thornton Road, and on Friday up the east side of Fethy Water as far as

Spulzieburn Farm. After this announcement we hear yet another innovation—the singing of a paraphrase from the *Translations and Paraphrases . . . of Sacred Scripture*, approved by the General Assembly in 1781. (Hymns outside this collection are not yet sung in the Established Church or in the Free Church, but the United Presbyterians in Kilmarkie began to use a hymn-book a few years ago.[43]) At the conclusion of the paraphrase the Minister pronounces the benediction with both arms extended. Just before the benediction we had heard a curious clicking sound along the central passage, and now we realize what it was: it was the unsnecking of pew doors. The man next to the passage in each pew had kept his hand on the door during the benediction, and immediately on the Minister's "Amen" he thrusts the door open, while the whole congregation (in the words of a contemporary writer) "stick on their hats and rush out as though the building were on fire[44]." During this stampede the Minister remains in his pulpit, then retires to the vestry, followed by the Beadle with the Bible and psalm-book. Perhaps the Minister wonders why the people should be in such haste to escape from the House of God; after all, the service was over in well under two hours—a much shorter time than when he was a boy.

No one stays to eat lunch in church, the interval before the afternoon service being rather longer than formerly. In Crocketbrig on the other hand there is only a short pause between the two services—enough for a little bite of food—and after the second service people get home to dinner about three. The afternoon service in Kilmarkie follows much the same pattern as that of the forenoon, but the Lord's prayer in not used, there is a shorter reading from Scripture, the second psalm is omitted; and the whole service lasts less than an hour and a half. In Tulloweir there is still no second service, nor is there in Traive, Braegunnion, or Kirkton of Glenderris. (Many churches in England are lit by gas and have an evening service, but this has not yet spread to Kilmarkie.[45])

The Lord's Supper is now observed in Kilmarkie once a year but with less intensity, and with far fewer secular accompaniments, than a hundred years before. Few visitors come from other parishes, for they all now have their own annual communions—indeed Carpoch now celebrates the Supper twice yearly; moreover the rise of the Free and United Presbyterian Churches has still further reduced the number of communicants, not only by drawing off many of the most devout to their own allegiance but also by making it easier for the undevout to belong to no church at all. The reduced scale of the solemnities means that the Minister of Kilmarkie can manage with the assistance of only two other ministers—his neighbour from Crocketbrig and an old college friend from Dumfries. Some such assistance, however, is required, for there is still a good deal of preaching to be done.

Thursday is still designated "Fast Day", but it is now little more than a secular holiday, though the pious devote it to preparation and there is general abstinence not only from work but from such pleasures as singing and whistling.[46] But though it is a secular holiday, the features of carnival that made the old celebrations a "holy fair" have almost entirely disappeared. The religious observances begin on Friday with a meeting in the church for prayer on behalf of those who are to officiate at the Sacrament. On Saturday two long addresses are given in the church, one in the forenoon, the other in the afternoon, at the end of which new communicants are admitted and tokens distributed. Outdoor meetings have been discontinued, for the audiences can all be accommodated within the kirk. But Kirkton of Glenderris, being nearer to the highlands where tradition dies harder, still holds tent-meetings on the Saturday and Monday. To that parish the old tradition is worth preserving merely to mark off the Sacrament as something very special; and out-of-doors preaching links the nineteenth-century church with the field conventicles of covenanting days, so that one can almost expect Claverhouse's dragoons to break the meeting up at any moment.[47]

The proceedings on Sabbath are much the same as a hundred years ago, but the service does not begin until eleven o'clock. The main or "action" sermon, lasting an hour, is preached by the visitor from Dumfries. The Minister of Kilmarkie "fences the table", but an invitation to the penitent to communicate is now much more prominent than the threat of damnation to unworthy recipients. The elders wear white cravats and swallow-tail coats; three of them bring in the elements—strips of white bread on silver plates and port wine in a tall silver cup; two others collect the communion tokens from those who have taken their seats at the table, for the long table is still set up in the central passage between the pews, but is no longer barricaded off to prevent anyone taking his seat without giving up his token. The ministers take it in turn to administer the Sacrament to relays of communicants, with a separate address and consecration for each "table". The bread and wine are passed from hand to hand in silence, and when each celebration is complete a plate is passed round in which offerings are placed for the poor. (The kirk door collections are now for church expenses, since the main responsibility for poor relief has been transferred to the civil authorities; but the kirk keeps its own fund for deserving cases known to the Minister and Session.) While the table is emptying and refilling, the whole congregation sings part of the 103rd Psalm, but there is some unseemly scrambling for places at the table by folk who want to get away early, e.g. to catch up on household duties.[48] Many leave the church after communicating, and thus miss the post-communion address. Those who stay the whole course will not get away until five o'clock. The Monday proceedings are likewise less elaborate, but there is an address in the forenoon, and in the afternoon the Minister of Kilmarkie "closes the work" with the customary summary of the preceding addresses, now known as a "purlicue".[49]

The foregoing is a description of worship in the parish kirk, but things are hardly any different in the other Presbyterian churches. The United Presbyterians, worshipping in the small Secession Church with plain round-arched windows which was built in 1812, are if anything a little more progressive than the "Auld Kirk". They abandoned the lining-out of the psalm some years ago and now conclude their worship with a hymn. The Free Church, in its plain Gothic building of 1846, is if anything a little more conservative: its prayers and sermons are a little longer than in the parish church, there are only two psalms, and the 103rd Psalm is still "lined-out" at the Communion.[50] In one respect, however, the Free Church is more advanced: at the Lord's Supper the communicants do not, nor did they ever, sit round a long table; instead they sit in pews which are covered with white linen "houseling" cloths for the occasion, and the bread and wine are carried to them by elders. It will be another ten years before the parish church adopts this practice.[51] The Episcopalians, worshipping in a small, rather elaborately decorated Gothic building of 1804, still use the English Book of Common Prayer but substitute the Scottish Communion Office of 1764 for the English form.

CHAPTER FIVE
1960

Again we slumber for another hundred years, and wake up in 1960. Once more we proceed to investigate the worship of Kilmarkie, and this time we are astonished at the changes that have taken place since 1860. It is as if nobody cared any longer for the principles, good or bad, which had determined the mode of Scottish worship from 1660 to 1860, and in accordance with which Scotsmen believed that theirs was the true, pure, scriptural method of worship, free from all taint of ritualism, emotionalism, aestheticism, and human inventions. Clearly some other principle is now in control.

There is again only one Presbyterian church in Kilmarkie. The former U.P. Church was turned into a cinema in 1921 and the former Free Church is now used by the "Assemblies of God". The parish church looks much the same from outside, but the interior has been rearranged to suit twentieth-century taste. In 1920, as a memorial to the fallen in the "Great War", the old pulpit (now in the Kilmarkie Museum) was replaced by a smaller and lower pulpit in light oak decorated with Celtic interlacing tracery; this is now situated at the north side of the east end. At the other side of the east end is the font (gifted in 1897 as a memorial to an honoured parishioner). The communion table (provided in 1872 when sitting round the long table was abandoned) now takes pride of place on a raised dais in the middle of the east end, with a shallow apse behind, ringed with beautifully carved elders' seats. In the south-east corner behind the font is an organ, erected after much controversy in 1883, and in front below the communion table are seats for the choir.

The morning service still begins at eleven o'clock, but nearly

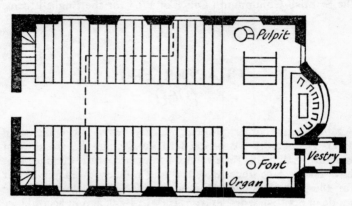

Dotted lines indicate gallery

everything else is different. There is no collection at the door (though this is still taken at the door in Tulloweir and Carpoch). As we enter, the organist is playing a voluntary, and we notice that the correct procedure on entering is to take off one's hat, if any, and to bow in prayer for a few moments on taking one's seat. At eleven the Beadle enters the pulpit carrying the Bible and the combined hymn-book and psalter. He is followed by the Minister, who wears not only a gown but also a cassock and his M.A. hood. He sits down in the pulpit and bows in prayer for a few moments. Then after the familiar "Let us worship

God", he announces a few verses of a psalm, which the congregation sing standing. The change from sitting to standing, and the corresponding change to sitting for the prayers, was made as long ago as 1870, but to us it is an innovation. At the end of the psalm the Minister calls the people to prayer with a verse or two of Scripture, and leads in prayer for five minutes; for the prayers the people have reverted to the seventeenth-century posture of sitting, and are probably quite unaware that this had been abandoned for some two hundred years before it was reintroduced in 1870. After the prayer a passage from the Old Testament is read, and after a hymn, a passage from the New Testament. Then a short address and a hymn for the children, a five-minute prayer of thanksgiving and intercession, concluding with the Lord's Prayer, in which the whole congregation joins. After another hymn comes the sermon, lasting only twenty minutes. This is followed by a short prayer, after which the Minister gives out the Intimations, to the effect that the Kirk Session will meet on Monday, the Woman's Guild on Wednesday, the Choir on Friday, and the Youth Club on Saturday. (There is now a hall alongside the kirk where all these activities can take place.) The collection is then taken—by means of plates passed along the pews by elders, who bring the offerings up to the communion table. The Minister, now standing behind the table, dedicates the offerings with a brief prayer, and then announces a Paraphrase, at the end of which he gives a benediction. The worshippers resume their seats and reverently bow in prayer for a few moments before filing unhurriedly out of the building. Meanwhile the Minister has gone to the kirk door to shake hands with all the worshippers as they leave. By the standards of former centuries the service is short, having lasted only an hour and a quarter.

The second service, now held in the evening at half past six, is similar but a little shorter. There is no Old Testament reading, no children's address, and one hymn fewer. It lasts about an hour.

The Lord's Supper is now observed quarterly, preceded only by a service of preparation on the previous Friday. The communicants no longer sit round a long table: since 1872 they have received the communion sitting in pews, and the bread and wine have been brought to them by elders. For this purpose they all sit together in the pews nearest the communion table. For some time the pews in which the communicants sat were covered with houseling cloths, but this custom has been discontinued. The communion bread has been diced into small cubes and the wine is drunk from small individual glasses handed round on special trays. (In Tulloweir and Crocketbrig, however, the wine is still drunk from large silver cups.) The elders wear dark suits and white ties.

The order of service is similar to that of 1860 except that there is no "fencing of the table" or any address from the communion table. (Until recently there was a brief "post-communion address", but this has been discontinued.) Tokens are no longer collected, but communion cards have been distributed beforehand by the elders, and are collected by elders as the communicants take their places for the communion. At the end of the service plates are passed round in which the communicants place an offering for the benevolent fund. The reduced scale of the celebration means that the Minister is able to conduct the entire service without assistance. It lasts well under two hours.

The episcopalians in Kilmarkie use the Scottish Book of Common Prayer, as published in 1929.

CHAPTER SIX
Baptisms, Marriages, Funerals

To complete this picture of Scottish worship, something ought
to be said about baptismal, marriage, and funeral services.

Baptisms
In 1560 the baptismal service in Kilmarkie followed the
form in the English prayer-book. Baptism was always
administered in church and in public, usually on the Lord's
Day, for private baptisms had been prohibited by law in order
to prevent baptism by popish priests. As compared with
baptisms under papistry, the reformed service was much
simplified, without spittle, candles, or salt. The service was
generally held at the end of afternoon worship, after which the
family party, with the godfathers and other friends, would
retire home, or to the alehouse, for as merry a dinner as they
could afford. The Minister remains in the pulpit for the
baptismal service, for as already noted the font, being carved
with idolatrous images, has been destroyed and its place has
been taken by a pewter basin which is placed, when required,
on a bracket attached to the pulpit. The baptism is effected by
the application of a little water to the child's face.

With the introduction of the Book of Common Order an
enlarged service was used, containing a long exhortation and
an even longer exposition of the Apostles' Creed, but otherwise
the previous customs continued, including the presence of
godfathers. In 1618 Parliament directed that baptism be
administered by the pouring of water over the child's head,
and the heritors accordingly purchased a laver—a pewter jug
from which the Minister poured the water over the child's
head as he held it over the basin. By 1660 the use of the laver

had been discontinued, and the service had become shorter again. The baptismal party, containing perhaps as many as twelve "witnesses", gathers round the foot of the pulpit; the Minister leads in prayer, and delivers a short address; he does not, of course, recite the Creed or require the father to do so, nor does he exact from him any vows or profession of faith: but this is unnecessary because some days previously the father had produced to the Session Clerk testimonials of witnesses to his worthiness, and then armed with a "ticket" from the Session Clerk had gone to the Minister to be examined as to his knowledge of the Christian faith, the Lord's Prayer, and the Ten Commandments. Without further ado, therefore, the father hands the child up to the Minister, who asks its name. "Alexander", says the father. "Alexander", says the Minister, "I baptize thee in the name of the Father, the Son, and the Holy Ghost", and applies a little water to the child's face. He then hands the baby down again to the father, who hands it back to the midwife. The Minister then admonishes the father and the witnesses as to their duties, and dismisses both the baptismal party and the congregation with the benediction.

In 1760 the procedure at baptisms was similar to that in 1660, except that most baptisms now took place in private houses. The change began in the early eighteenth century with requests from the gentry, who found that church attendance on the baptismal day interfered with the social occasion. As it was difficult for the Minister to refuse a request from an influential laird, it became impossible to refuse requests from more humble folk also. Besides, week-day baptisms avoided the desecration of the Sabbath which would be incurred by the surrounding festivities. In so far as the Sacrament is administered in church, a laver is again in use in Kilmarkie: it was gifted to the kirk in 1695, but by 1760 it is used, not for pouring water over the child's head, but for pouring water into the basin at the beginning of the service.[52] By 1860, in Kilmarkie at least, although most baptisms are administered in houses, baptism in church is no longer rare, though sometimes the church service takes place privately on a week-day.[53]

(This return to the church is partly because the accompanying social celebrations are now less elaborate.) If the baptism is on a Sabbath, it takes place immediately after the sermon, often at the morning service. The Minister begins with an address to the father and witnesses, and asks the father if he assents to the obligations thus described; the father bows his head in acknowledgment; the Minister then offers prayer, after which the baptism proceeds as before. The laver is no longer used. By 1960, although some baptisms are still administered privately, most baptisms in Kilmarkie take place in church at the end of morning worship. Although in some town churches the Minister recites the Creed in the course of the baptismal service, this practice has not yet been introduced in Kilmarkie; but the parents (the baptism is now deferred until the mother can be present too) are required to profess their Christian faith and to promise to bring the child up "in the nurture and admonition of the Lord".

Marriages[54]

Marriages in 1560 were solemnized in Kilmarkie according to the English prayer-book during public worship on Sunday, usually before the sermon. This practice continued under the Book of Common Order, though in the seventeenth century the marriage was usually after rather than before the sermon. During that century, however, opposition developed to Sunday marriages because the social festivities and the work of preparing for them involved a profanation of the Lord's Day; hence the recommendation of the Westminster Divines in the Directory for Public Worship: "We advise that it be not on the Lord's day". Thus in Kilmarkie by 1660 most marriages, though solemnized in church, took place on a week-day. The blessing and giving of a ring had been abandoned as superstitious, nor was it any longer necessary that the parties to the marriage should repeat the Lord's Prayer, the Belief, and the Ten Commandments. At the beginning of the eighteenth century the gentry began marrying in private houses; at first kirk sessions used to fine them for this, but gradually the clergy yielded to social pressure and were more and more ready to conduct marriage services out of church. By 1760 no one gets married in the kirk of Kilmarkie unless he is too poor to afford a celebration at home. By 1860 no one gets married in church at all. Kilmarkie folk who cannot afford a celebration at the Plenish Arms Hotel or the Mitchell Institute get married quietly at home. Soon after 1860, however, the tide began to turn. Reformers pleaded that so solemn a ceremony ought to take place in the House of God, not at a scene of festivity; at the same time church services were requested by fashionable folk who aped Anglican ways. By 1960 church-going people in Kilmarkie normally get married in church, though the wedding sometimes takes place in the vestry if special circumstances, e.g. a recent bereavement, make a public wedding inappropriate. The minister is however often asked by people less closely connected with the church to conduct a ceremony at the Plenish Arms or wherever the wedding reception is to be held.

Funerals

The changing history of funeral customs is perhaps even more remarkable than that of baptisms and marriages. In 1560 funerals usually took place on a Sunday. In Kilmarkie whenever a death occurred the bellman went about the town ringing his hand-bell and at strategic points calling out "Faithful brethren and sisters, I let you to wot that there is a faithful brother [or sister] lately departed out of this present world, as it hath pleased Almighty God. He [or she] was called . . . and lived in . . .". A day or two later the bellman goes about again to notify the hour and house where neighbours may meet to attend the deceased to the place of burial. On the day of burial the corpse is carried to the kirkyard in the common coffin, covered with the black parish mortcloth; the chief mourners walk in front of the coffin, others follow, and women come last.[55] When the cortege reaches the kirkyard the corpse is taken out of the coffin and lowered into the grave. The graveside service in Kilmarkie follows generally that in the English prayer-book, but instead of psalms there is sung the hymn from the *Gude and Godlie Balatis* beginning "Our brother lat vs put in graue".[56]

. We were just in time to experience a funeral service at Kilmarkie in 1560, for very soon afterwards all funeral services were discontinued, lest encouragement be given to popish practices such as masses or prayers for the dead. All that was permitted by the Book of Common Order (1562) was that after the burial the minister might go to the church and make "some profitable exhortation to the people touching death and resurrection". The prohibition[57] of funeral services (repeated by the General Assembly in 1638) was strictly observed in Scotland for more than two hundred years. In 1660 the preliminaries continue with little alteration except that the words "as it hath pleased Almighty God" are omitted from the bellman's announcement, to stop him from observing the popish custom of taking off his bonnet at the mention of the Divine name. The cortege proceeds on its way as before, except that the bellman rings no bell in front of it and the kirk bell is no longer tolled as it enters the kirkyard; these usages are now thought to be superstitious. Last year when old Craik of Dowie died the Minister of Kilmarkie was induced to preach a funeral sermon for him, but this was the first such sermon in this district since 1634,[58] and ordinary folk are buried without any kind of religious ceremony. Things are exactly the same in 1760, except that even funeral sermons are now entirely obsolete; but by 1860 a change has set in. Early in the nineteenth century religion began to be associated once more with funerals. The change did not come through reforming ministers attempting to introduce formal services: an attempt of that kind was made in St. Andrew's Church, Glasgow, in 1807, but had to be given up because the public reaction was so hostile. The change grew rather from quite small beginnings. To encourage the linen and woollen industries Acts had been passed imposing the use of linen and then woollen shrouds, and to enforce this the nearest elder, with a neighbour or two, was required to see the body put into the "kist". This "coffining" gradually developed into a social occasion, at which cake with wine or whisky was handed round to the mourners. Later it became the custom to ask the Minister to attend as well as elder, and of course he was asked to say a blessing on the refreshments, and the blessing developed into a prayer, and the prayer into a full-blown funeral service with Scripture readings and an address.[59] By 1860 in Kilmarkie such a service is often held in the house on the day of the funeral before the cortege sets out for the kirkyard. Sometimes a service is added at the grave-side. By 1960 it is normal to hold both a short service in the house and a very short service at the grave-side. Not often is there a service in the church, and the cemetery (which has superseded the kirkyard) has no chapel.

CHAPTER SEVEN
2060

Sometimes a historian goes out of his strict province and offers a commentary on the events he has recounted. It is no part of the intention of this booklet to suggest what changes may be desirable in the present worship of the Church of Scotland. It may however be of some use to set down a few conclusions which seem to emerge from the foregoing narrative; they may be worth bearing in mind by those who seek either to introduce or to oppose future changes.

1. Some periods are times of rapid change; at others custom settles into a style which changes only slowly. Examples of the former type are the years 1640–60 and 1870–1900; of the latter, the years 1700–1840. On this contrast the following interesting comment was made a century and a half ago by Lockhart:

The modes of public worship are matters of such solemn usage, that they seldom undergo any sober, considerate, or partial alterations. They are left untouched, except in times when the passions of mankind are very deeply and terribly stirred, or when great revolutions of opinion take place—and then they are changed with a mad and headlong zeal—and certainly there would be something very like indecent quackery, in rashly shifting about the forms of worshipping God, according to the mutable tastes of each successive generation.[60]

2. Sometimes a new practice long outlives the reasons for its introduction, and becomes so deeply entrenched that it cannot be abandoned without bitter controversy. Examples can be found from the customs established in the sixteenth century to guard against Roman abuses, or in the seventeenth in the illusory hope of uniformity with England.

3. Some reforms cannot be brought about except by bold pioneers who risk being abused as enemies of the Church; others must wait for the slow but irresistible forces of social pressure and changing taste. But without some assistance from these forces even the most courageous of pioneers is powerless; that is perhaps why Lee, although he persuaded the Church to install organs, sing hymns, and stand for singing, was unable to induce any but his own congregation to kneel for prayer.

4. Small changes often pass unnoticed (it is often difficult to discover from contemporary records just when they began), but when they are all added up the difference over a hundred years can be very great.

To illustrate this last point, let us imagine that in 1960 we went to sleep for another hundred years and that we waken up in Kilmarkie in the year 2060. What follows is not intended as a picture of what is *likely* to be normal then (no predictions can be made in such an uncertain realm), nor of what the writer necessarily considers *desirable*; the object is simply to show what kind of changes are easily *possible* within a hundred years if the pace of change is no greater than in the century 1860–1960.

Many changes meet our eye as we approach the parish church. The nineteenth-century building, destroyed in 1991 by a stray rocket from the Faroe Islands, has been replaced

41

by a structure resembling in external appearance part of a nuclear power station. Inside it is of circular plan with a round communion table in the middle of a circular central area, underneath which is a cruciform baptistery which can be opened up by removal of the floorboards. (The baptistery is needed for the not infrequent ceremonies of baptism administered to people brought up in the Assembly of God or outside the Christian faith. Modern practice, while permitting the sprinkling of babies, requires the immersion of adults.) Around this central plain the pews rise in tiers right round the church except at one point where there is the pulpit and a space opposite where there is the orchestra. Organs are out of fashion again, the singing being accompanied by a small amateur orchestra of recorders, saxophones, and drums. The drum features prominently in the worship, having been introduced by the evangelists from Malawi who led the revival of 2012. Below the pulpit is the Reader's desk, and in front of the orchestra the font. There are no windows: the church is lit by electric light and the walls are covered with mural paintings illustrating the Apostles' Creed.

The Sunday morning service begins at 9 o'clock, and the first half-hour of worship is conducted by a Reader, who is one of the elders. The service follows the Scottish National Prayer-book of 2006, similar in general outline to that in the Anglican prayer-book of 1988, but differing considerably in detail. The prayers are of formal type which a minister may vary but from which a reader only selects. The service begins with a sentence or two of Scripture, and then proceeds to a general confession of sins, based on that in Knox's Book of Common Order; this is said by the whole congregation, kneeling. Then is sung a psalm, from the new metrical version of 2018, to one of the African tunes. This is followed by the Old Testament reading, a hymn, the New Testament reading; the Apostles' Creed (said by all, standing), the Scottish collect for the day, various short prayers of thanksgiving, supplication, and intercession, and a short litany punctuated by drum-beats. Then follows a period in which anyone present may lead in prayer or ask for prayer for a particular object. Today a not

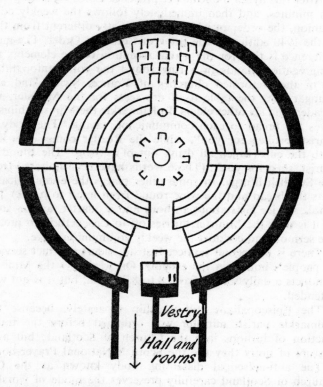

Vestry

Hall and
rooms

unusual phenomenon occurs at this point: someone stands up and speaks in a "tongue". Immediately the Reader calls for interpretation, and one of the elders, who has the gift of interpretation, expounds briefly the meaning of the ecstatic utterance. After this another hymn is sung, during which the Minister enters, wearing a blue surplice. He could not come earlier because he was conducting the weekly communion at Carpoch. (Owing to the chronic shortage of ministers it is quite common for one minister to be in charge of three or more parishes, assisted by a deaconess and readers.)

43

After this hymn the Minister preaches a sermon lasting only ten minutes, and then immediately follows the weekly communion, the order of which is not greatly different from that in the 1940 edition of the Book of Common Order. The main difference is that for the actual reception of the elements the congregation stands in a ring round the communion table, as in the Reformed churches of France, Switzerland and Hungary. At the table itself are seats for the Minister, the Reader, and six other elders. In Kilmarkie the Minister himself gives the bread to each communicant, saying "The Body of Christ, broken for you", while the Reader comes after him with the cup (which all drink out of) saying "The Blood of Christ, shed for you". (These words have been imitated from the Swedish liturgy. In some other places the communicants pass the bread and the wine round from hand to hand.) The whole service lasts about an hour and a quarter, and as soon as it is over the Minister hurries off to Crocketbrig to preach the sermon and conduct the weekly communion there.

There is no second service. Instead, elders conduct services in people's houses in the evening. On weekdays the Minister conducts a daily service from 8 to 8.30 a.m., but it is not well attended.

The Episcopalians still worship separately, because the Kilmarkie parish minister was ordained before the introduction of bishops into the Church of Scotland; but as a gesture of unity they use the Scottish National Prayer-book.

The anti-episcopal dissenting body known as the Old Church of Scotland carefully preserves the mode of worship characteristic of the Church of Scotland in the last quarter of the twentieth century. In the Church of Scotland itself, though many changes have taken place in the last hundred years, the experts are still convinced that its worship is more truly Presbyterian than ever it was before.

BIBLIOGRAPHY

Boyd, A. K. H.: *Lessons of Middle Age*, London, 1868 (chapters IV and VII).

Burnet, G. B.: *The Holy Communion in the Reformed Church of Scotland*, Edinburgh, 1960.

Burns, Thomas: *Old Scottish Communion Plate*, Edinburgh, 1892.

Edgar, Andrew: *Old Church Life in Scotland*, Paisley, 1885 (I) and 1886 (II).

Farmer, H. G.: *A History of Music in Scotland*, London, 1947.

Fraser, Duncan: *The Passing of the Precentor*, Edinburgh, 1906.

Gibson, W. Milne: *The Old Scottish Precentor*, Aberdeen, 1907.

Graham, Henry Grey: *Social Life in Scotland in the Eighteenth Century*, London, 1899 (chapters VIII and IX).

Hay, George: *The Architecture of Scottish Post-Reformation Churches*, Oxford, 1957.

Henderson, G. D.: *Religious Life in Seventeenth-Century Scotland*, Cambridge, 1937 (chapters I and VII).

Jamieson, Robert: Article on the Church of Scotland in *Cyclopaedia of Religious Denominations*, Glasgow, 1853. (Jamieson was minister of St. Paul's, Glasgow, and subsequently Moderator of the General Assembly; for other writings of his see D.N.B.)

Lee, Robert: *The Reform of the Church of Scotland*, Part I, Edinburgh, 1964; reprinted 1966.

Leishman, Thomas: *The Ritual of the Church of Scotland*, forming pages 307-431 of vol. V of *The Church of Scotland, Past and Present*, edited by R. H. Story, London, 1891. (Quoted in the following notes simply as "Leishman", except where this has to be distinguished from his work on the Directory of Public Worship, when the former is designated "Leishman in Story V" and the latter "Leishman on the Directory".)

—— Commentary on the Directory for Public Worship: see under Sprott.

McCrie, C. G.: *The Public Worship of Presbyterian Scotland*, Edinburgh, 1892.

McMillan, W.: *The Worship of the Scottish Reformed Church, 1550-1638*, London, 1931.

Maxwell, W. D.: *A History of Worship in the Church of Scotland*, 1955.

Patrick, Miller: *Four Centuries of Scottish Psalmody*, Oxford, 1949.

Philp, R. K. (Editor): *The Denominational Reason Why*, London, 1860. (The description of worship in the Church of Scotland is largely abridged from Jamieson.)

Sands, Lord: *The Order and Conduct of Divine Service in the Church of Scotland* (pamphlet), Edinburgh, 1923.

Sprott, G. W.: *The Worship and Offices of the Church of Scotland*, Edinburgh, 1882.

—— *The Worship of the Church of Scotland during the Covenanting Period*, 1638-61 (Lee Lecture), Edinburgh, 1893.

—— and Leishman, T.: *The Book of Common Order and Directory for the Public Worship of God*, with Historical Introductions and Illustrative Notes, Edinburgh, 1868. (The Book of Common Order is handled by Sprott, the Directory by Leishman.)

Story, R. H.: *The Life and Remains of Robert Lee*, London, 1870, volume I, chapter XI; volume II, chapters II and IV. (See also under Leishman.)

Wright, Alexander: *The Presbyterian Church, its Worship, Functions and Ministerial Orders*, Edinburgh, 1895.

NOTES

1. This was certainly the seventeenth-century practice (McMillan, p. 160), and I assume it continued from before the Reformation. Similarly I assume that the Reformation habit of kneeling for prayer during Divine worship was a continuation of existing practice, since there was no controversy on the matter except as regards the reception of Holy Communion. Oddly, however, David Calderwood in the next century, in the preface to his *Historie of the Kirk of Scotland*, lists "not to kneele upon the Lord's day in time of prayer" among the superstitious rites which entered the Kirk many centuries before the Reformation (Wodrow Society Edition, i. 38).

2. It is certain that the English Prayer-book was extensively used at this time in the larger towns; for instance Kirkcaldy of Grange writing to Cecil on 29th July 1559 said—

> As to paroys churchis they cleyne them of ymages and all other monumentis of ydolatrie, and commands that no Messis be said in them: in place therof the Booke sett fourthe be godlye Kyng Edward is red in the same churches. (Quoted in John Knox's *Works*, ed. Laing, vi, 34.)

Other evidence will be found in Knox's Works, i, 275, 299-300; vi, 22, 277, 279. See also A. F. Mitchell, *The Scottish Reformation* (1890), pp. 128-32; H. J. Wotherspoon, *The Second Prayer-Book of King Edward the Sixth* (1905), pp. 33-54, 61-62; McMillan, pp. 33-35; Gordon Donaldson, *The Scottish Reformation* (1960), p. 49; Jasper Ridley, *John Knox* (1968), p. 328. It seems safe enough to assume that the use of the English Prayer-book had penetrated to Kilmarkie, though how closely it was followed is quite uncertain. Indeed much of the actual usage in 1560 must be left to conjecture, the evidence being so scanty: hence the uncertainty of some of the following notes.

3. There is no positive evidence that this or any other items from the *Gude and Godlie Ballatis* were sung in church services; but then there is no evidence that anything else was sung before the publication of the *Scottish Psalter*: and yet it is inconceivable that Scottish reformed churches, alone in Europe, would sing neither psalms nor hymns nor spiritual songs when meeting together for worship (1 Cor. 14: 26; Eph. 5: 19). It is known that the *Gude and Godlie Ballatis* were popular in the 1540's and 1550's (see A. F. Mitchell's edition published for the Scottish Text Society, 1897, p. xxxix; Miller Patrick, pp. 5-6); they are expressly stated as intended to be sung (Mitchell's edition, p. 85); many are translations from German

47

D

originals which were intended to be sung in church as well as at home (ibid., p. lii). McMillan (p. 22) thinks that about this time one of the devotional hymns from this collection would often be included in a church service, though the psalms would more probably be sung from Sternhold and Hopkins. Jasper Ridley (*John Knox*, p. 328) even thinks that in their anti-Roman zeal congregations would sing in church satirical verses to popular tunes, such as "The Paip, that Pagane full of pryde", with its jaunty refrain "Hay trix, tryme go trix, vnder the grene wod tre". I doubt this, and have taken the more cautious line of confining Kilmarkie usage to the Belief and the psalms. It seems to me likely that many parishes would use just the one book and not trouble themselves with an English psalter when they had a fair selection in Scots in the Book of Ballatis.

4. According to the note to Psalm 150, verse 3, in the Geneva Bible (1560), the psalmist "maketh mention of those instruments, which by God's commandment were appointed in the old Law, but under Christ the use thereof is abolished in the Church." At the beginning of the Reformation in Scotland, however, some organs, where they existed at all, were allowed to continue in use for a time, and a few places had other instruments such as shawms and fifes, though there seems to be no evidence of their actual use in ordinary worship except in such places as Chapels Royal (McMillan, chap. VII).

5. It seems a reasonable inference from the Act of Assembly of 1575 forbidding ministers and readers to wear gaudy clothes or to wear plaids when officiating in the kirk, that ecclesiastical garb was not generally used at that time, and the position would seem to have been much the same when James VI, by authority of Parliament, ordained in 1609 that ministers should wear black gowns in the pulpit. But it is known that academic gowns were regularly worn by Knox and other Reformed ministers in Scotland and elsewhere, and what they wore in the street they probably wore in the pulpit also. The scanty evidence is given in W. D. Maxwell, *John Knox's Genevan Service Book* (1931), p. 212, R. A. S. Macalister, *Ecclesiastical Vestments* (1896), Sprott (B.C.O.), p. lvi, and McMillan, pp. 364-65; cf. Sprott, *The Worship and Offices of the Church of Scotland* (1882), pp. 243-44.

Even the papistical clergy had been casual about the wearing of distinctive clerical dress, at least outside church, for it was necessary for Archbishop Betoun in 1559 to enjoin his clergy to wear suitable clothing (*habitus decens*) to distinguish themselves from the laity (*Melrose Regality Records*, printed in Scottish History Society 2nd series, xiii, 183-84). On the other hand scholars at this time wore black cloaks, sometimes tipped with fur, and it would be natural for a Reformed minister to wear such. The Minister of Tranent, who died in 1569, had among his property two black gowns, and bequeathed one of them—"my black furrit gown"—to the vicar of Tranent, presumably a pre-Reformation priest who was not acting in the reformed Church. (Edinburgh Testaments, 20th October 1569.)

6. In 1573 the General Assembly forbad the taking of collections otherwise than at the church door. No doubt practice varied considerably before then. It would be natural for congregations using the English Prayer-book to take the collection during the service at the point directed by the book. The box on the end of a pole, known later as a "ladle", was used by English Presbyterians and was introduced into some Scottish churches in the eighteenth and nineteenth centuries. There is no positive evidence for its use in the sixteenth century, but it is very likely that some such device was adopted for collection of the offerings from a mass of worshippers squatting on stools, benches, or the ground.

7. See McCrie, pp. 443-44. The General Assembly in 1562 ordained the communion to be ministered four times a year in the burghs, and twice a year in the country parishes. In the Kirk of the Canongate from 1565 the Lord's Supper was celebrated three times a year; it is unlikely to have been observed more than twice a year in Kilmarkie.

8. The relative duties of elders and deacons were not clearly distinguished at this time; not every parish had both; but it was considered appropriate that the "serving of tables" should be done by deacons, because service of tables (though of a different kind) had been assigned in Acts 6: 1-6 to the Seven (who may not have been deacons).

9. The reasons are thus succinctly stated by James MacGregor in his preface to Thomas Burns's book (p. xi): "The old Communion plate was not fitted for the Communion service of the Reformed Church. A cup which was meant to contain just enough wine for one person to drink was not fitted for use where wine was to be given to every communicant. Nor was a paten or pix, made to hold wafers, suitable for use where common bread, and a large quantity of it, was to be used." Actually, as Burns himself makes clear (p. 16), little shortbread cakes were more often used at this time, but for these also the pix would have been unsuitable.

49

10. The communion procedure described here represents the normal practice under the Book of Common Order in the later 1560's. How much of it dates back to 1560 is a matter for conjecture. We have no positive evidence.

11. For Sang Schules see Miller Patrick, pp. 109 and 129-30.

12. Jamieson thought the Lettergae was the one who *let gae* the line (i.e. "lined it out"), and his Dictionary quotes Forbes's *Dominie Depos'd* in support of this interpretation. But the word was in use long before lining out was introduced, and seems to have given rise to the expression "let gae the line" rather than vice versa. The better explanation is that Lettergae is a pre-Reformation title and meant "liturgy-man".

13. For a full and exact account see Sprott's Lee Lecture.

14. See notes 26 and 27 below.

15. For this paragraph see Hay, pp. 168, 184-85, 219-20, 195-96, 28, 199; and Edgar (I), pp. 11-29, 290-93.

16. Leishman, pp. 329-31; Sprott, *The Worship and Offices of the Church of Scotland*, pp. 17-20.

17. Evidence is lacking as to the point in the service at which the Minister gave the intimations, of which specimens are described also under 1760 and 1860. When there was a Reader, they would have been given out by him before the Minister entered. In later times intimations were sometimes made by the Precentor, e.g. that prayer was requested for certain sick persons mentioned by name; this was doubtless done by the Precentor in his capacity as successor to the vanished Reader. In recent times banns of marriage have often been called at the outset of the service. It is assumed that this is a survival of an ancient practice, and that from the seventeenth century all intimations would be made at this point. See also notes 28 and 39 below.

18. "Let persons relapse in Adultery (or above) quadrilapse in Fornication (or above) or often guilty of other grosser scandals, be Excommunicat somewhat more summarly [i.e. emphatically] than in an ordinary processe . . . both for the hainousness of the Sins and continuance therein, and also for terrour to others; And these not to be relaxed from the sentence of Excommunication without evidence, and undeniable signes of Repentance."—From Act of General Assembly, 10th August 1648.

19. There is a good description of the exercise of discipline from the pulpit in Maxwell, pp. 145-55. See also Edgar (I), pp. 286-305.

20. A writer in 1705 (Hog, Minister of Carnock) condemned the repetition of the Lord's words as "a manifest prostitution of them, and a downright turning of all into a lifeless, sapless, and loathsome form"; those who are exercised in godliness would, he thought, agree that the use of the Lord's Prayer in worship was "an engine of hell, not only far contrary to the divine prescript, but likewise perversive to the Gospel of Christ". (Quoted by Leishman, p. 400.)

21. The writer of the Episcopalian satire *The Scotch Presbyterian Eloquence* (1692) was hardly fair in the contrast he made (in his "Short Catechism") between the Presbyterian attitudes to the Lord's Prayer and the Creed.

> "Q.—Why do not the Presbyterians say the creed and the doxology?
> A.—Because they are not word by word in Scripture.
> Q.—Why do they not say the Lord's prayer?
> A.—Because it is word by word in Scripture."

22. For descriptions of communion services about this time see Leishman on the Directory, pp. 267, 348-49; Leishman in Story, V, pp. 390-91; McMillan, pp. 196-97, 229; Maxwell, pp. 122-23; Henderson, pp. 155-56; Burnet chap. VIII. In some places there were larger crowds, more ministers, more outdoor preaching, and longer services; elsewhere the new customs had not yet taken hold.

23. Burns, p. 63.

24. See for instance T. Smith, *Memoirs of James Begg, D.D.* (1885), Vol. I, pp. 22-23.

25. A graphic account of the distribution of the bread in New Aberdeen in September 1643 is given by Spalding in his *Memorialls of the Trubles*, II, p. 279. In contrast to the previous practice under episcopacy, the bread—

> wes baikin in ane round loof lyk ane trynscheour, syne cuttit out in long scheives hanging be ane tak; and, first, the minister takis ane scheive, eftir the blissing, and brakis ane peice and gives to him who is narrest, and he gives the scheive to his nightbour, who takis ane peice and syne gives it to his nichtbour, whill it be spent; and syne ane elder gives in ane vther scheive whair the first scheive left, and so furth."

26. Sir Walter Scott (e.g. in *Old Mortality* and *The Bride of Lammermoor*) was mistaken in thinking that the English Prayer-book was used in parish churches during this period. There is some evidence of limited use in Chapels Royal and private families (see

51

Records of the Scottish Church History Society, IV, 145-49), but even Episcopalians did not use the Prayer-book in public worship until about 1712. In some dioceses attempts were made, with some success, to restore the Creed to use, and to reappoint Readers to give out the first psalm and read the Scriptures. Cf. Maxwell, pp. 112-18.

27. A curious exception is the posture adopted for prayer. Standing, which at the end of the seventeenth century was favoured rather by Episcopalians, came to be generally adopted during the eighteenth century as the standard Presbyterian custom, while the Episcopalians took to kneeling. Cf. Leishman, p. 401.

28. Briefs of this kind were read several times a year in most parishes: see W. A. Bewes, *Church Briefs* (1896), and G. D. Henderson, *Scottish Ruling Elder* (1935), pp. 97-98. For Kilmarkie I have transposed a few months back an actual appeal promulgated in 1761 by command of Royal letters patent dated 24th October 1760: see Bewes, pp. 252-54, 328. I have allotted the reading to the Precentor for the reasons given in note 17.

29. See note 26. The partial reintroduction of the Reader's Service and the abandonment of the sitting posture for prayers (note 27) are all that Scotland managed to salvage from the puritan invasion. In some parishes in the eighteenth century, particularly in the Highlands, the Precentor or other elders read from the Scriptures while the congregation assembled, before the opening psalm was sung.

30. For descriptions of worship about 1760 see Leishman, pp. 420-421; Graham, pp. 278-79, 290-91; Maxwell, pp. 139-40. For a hostile contemporary description by an Episcopalian see McCrie, pp. 310-12; a similar account is given in a pamphlet of 1723 entitled *The CAUSES of the DECAY of Presbytery in Scotland.* . . . The description in *Rob Roy* (chap. XX) of the service in Glasgow Cathedral gives a fair account of early eighteenth-century worship, though of course there were more items in the service than the psalm, prayer, and sermon which are all that Scott describes. Exact accounts will be found of a service in Edinburgh in 1788 in Joseph Farington's notes (reproduced in *The Scotsman*, 6th February 1935) and of worship in Rothiemurchus in 1812-13 in Elizabeth Grant's *Memoirs of a Highland Lady* (ed. Lady Strachey, 1898). These, however, cannot be applied directly to Kilmarkie, not so much because they are well after 1760 (practice changed little at this period), but because city and highland practice often differed considerably from that of the middle lowlands.

31. Cf. T. Smith, *Memoirs of James Begg, D.D.* (1885), vol. I, p. 23.

32. For descriptions of eighteenth-century communions see Leishman on the Directory, p. 349; Leishman in Story V, p. 410; Graham, pp. 302-14; Maxwell, pp. 141-45; Burnet, pp. 217-32. There is a good contemporary description of an Edinburgh communion service in John Wesley's Diary for 16th June 1764; his account is objective, but he concludes with the comment "How much more simple, as well as more solemn, is the service of the Church of England!" (Oddly enough it was the simplicity and solemnity of the Scottish communion service that led Queen Victoria to prefer it to the English. See *More Leaves from the Journal of a Life in the Highlands,* 13th November 1871.) Robert Burns's *Holy Fair* (descriptive of the communion season at Mauchline about 1785) is probably not far from the truth, but is concerned rather with the social and secular than with the devotional aspects of the "occasion", and it is not clear how much of what Burns describes is supposed to take place within the church and how much outside. A more comprehensive account of a sacramental occasion (from a rather later but not greatly different period) is to be found in *Peter's Letters to his Kinsfolk* (by J. G. Lockhart, third edition, 1819), letters LXXV, LXXVI, LXXVII.

33. *The Holy Communion in the Reformed Church of Scotland,* pp. 249, 219-20.

34. See Lockhart's book quoted in note 32 above, vol. III, pp. 318-19.

35. See John Mitchell's *Memories of Ayrshire* in the *Miscellany* of the Scottish Church History Society, vol. VI (1939), pp. 310, 331-32; Tait, *Border Church Life,* vol. II (1891), p. 249 describes a Secession service of 1772 lasting from 11 a.m. to 2 p.m.

36. The order of worship in the middle of the nineteenth century has not been so well written up as that of preceding centuries. I have relied principally on Jamieson, pp. 97-106, Lee, pp. 12-13 and 171, and the Report of the special committee to the General Assembly of 1864. Lord Sands pp. 16-18 is also valuable, but as he was recording in 1923 what he remembered of his boyhood in the 'sixties he cannot be absolutely relied on. Useful contemporary accounts of particular orders of service will be found in Henry Caswall, *Scotland and the Scottish Church* (Oxford, 1853), p. 102 (recent description by a highland minister) and R. H. Story's *Life and Remains of Robert*

Lee, vol. I, p. 329. Lee on pp. 12-13 said there was great variety, but the 1864 report set out an order of worship which it stated was followed "almost universally". As this is supported by the other authorities quoted, and represents a middle course between the variations described by Lee and Lord Sands, I have followed it closely in the account of Kilmarkie.

37. Evidence for times of services is hard to come by, but a writer in the English Journal *The Presbyterian* for 1st August 1868 said "In most of our Scotch towns there is forenoon service at eleven, and afternoon service at two or a quarter past two. In rural districts the congregation meets at mid-day, either for one long diet of worship, or two short ones, with a brief interval between; while in some places there is forenoon and evening service." Eleven o'clock was the time of service in 1843 in Kilsyth, Woodside (Aberdeen), and Glasgow (St Andrew's) (Thomas Brown, *Annals of the Disruption*); it was the same in distant Scalloway in 1854 (G. M. Nelson, *The Story of Tingwall Kirk*, 1965, p. 64), in St. Andrews in 1868 (Boyd, p. 95), in Gardenstown in 1872 (J. Boyd Primmer, *Life of Jacob Primmer*, 1916, p. 22), and in Townhill in 1876 (ibid., p. 33). At Balmoral in 1854 and 1855 (as Queen Victoria recorded in her *Leaves from the Journal of our Life in the Highlands* on 29th and 14th October respectively) the service began at twelve o'clock, but highland practice was probably different then, as it still is.

38. Lee, chap. VI.

39. Lord Sands (p. 17) says that in the 1860's banns of marriage were proclaimed by the Precentor before the service began, while other intimations were generally made before the last psalm.

40. "The Lettergae" in *Hamewith*, by Charles Murray. It would seem that lining-out began to be modified or abandoned towards the middle of the nineteenth century, but all changes in what had become a national institution were strongly opposed by conservative elements and it took a long time to die out. Leishman, McCrie, and Wright are agreed that by the 1890's it survived only in the highlands. For a time it was retained in the lowlands for the psalm sung at communion "between tables", but even this died away when the long table gave way to service of the whole congregation in their pews at one sitting. Lee (pp. 28-29) seems to have been under the impression that lining-out had been universally abandoned by 1864, but if so he cannot have been fully informed, for Gibson (p. 34) tells a story of a protest from the gallery "not quite fifty years ago" (i.e.

soon after 1867) when a new precentor was instructed not to "read the line".

In some places the method of "reading the line" seems to have been modified before the custom was dropped altogether. In a church in Aberdeen in 1830 it was decided to read two lines at a time (Millar Patrick, p. 190); the painter Millais heard the line read at Glenfinlas in 1855, but according to his description the precentor chanted only the first line of the verse, after which the whole verse was sung by the congregation (ibid., p. 142). Sometimes the line, instead of being chanted in monotone, was literally "read" in ordinary speech: this is evidently what Charles Murray's Lettergae did, for he did not pitch the note until after he had read the line; Gibson (p. 187) tells a story of a nineteenth-century candidate for a precentorship who could sing well but failed because owing to a stammer he could not "read the line". Reading of the line would also give some plausibility to the story of the precentor who after announcing a common metre tune said "It is so dark I canna see", whereupon the congregation sang those words to the first line of the tune; the story continues, less plausibly, that the precentor then said "I canna see at a' ", which the congregation then sang to the second line, after which the congregation dutifully sang to the third and fourth lines his exclamations "I think the people have gone mad" and "The devil take them a' ".

The best estimate I can make is that by 1860 many congregations in the big towns, and some in the country, had abandoned the lining-out; in others it was retained in a modified form; and in many others, particularly in the country, the old fashion continued. Kilmarkie, as usual, follows the middle course.

41. It may be useful to summarize the main facts here, since they are not always correctly stated in histories of Scottish worship.

The use of the organ in Scottish Presbyterian worship began with the introduction by Dr. Robert Lee of a harmonium into the Kirk of the Greyfriars, Edinburgh. Previously there had been organs in some episcopal chapels as early as the eighteenth century (Farmer, pp. 272-73); in 1845 an Independent congregation in Edinburgh purchased an organ for use in their service (J. R. Fleming, *A History of the Church in Scotland, 1843-1874* (1927), p. 117). An attempt had been made by Dr. Ritchie in 1807 to transfer to St. Andrew's Church, Glasgow, an organ which had been installed for secular purposes in a disused part of the Cathedral, but the Town Council refused permission.

In the same year, 1863, an Overture came to the General Assembly from the Synod of Aberdeen, asking the Assembly to "secure as far as possible uniformity in the forms of public worship within the Church". It was not the harmonium but other innovations (particularly at Greyfriars) that occasioned the Overture, but the Committee set up by the Assembly to consider the whole subject made mention of organs in the report which it presented to the Assembly in the following year. The motion which was carried in the Assembly that year implied that innovations in worship could be tolerated if they would not impair the harmony of particular congregations or disturb the peace of the Church in general.

Immediately the Rev. Ranald McPherson, not satisfied with this, raised in the Presbytery of Edinburgh the whole question of the Greyfriars innovations (including the harmonium as well as such matters as read prayers and kneeling for prayer). After debate, the Previous Question was carried. Mr. McPherson appealed to the Synod, which dismissed the appeal, and he thereupon took his case to the Assembly. In the Assembly (1865) Dr. Pirie, without referring explicitly to instrumental music, introduced a motion to the effect that all arrangements with regard to public worship are subject to regulation by Presbyteries; this was carried by 173 votes to 140 against a counter-motion which would have left such matters to Kirk Sessions. In view of this decision Mr. McPherson's appeal was dismissed. Meanwhile a pipe organ had been installed in the newly built church at Anderston, Glasgow, which was opened for public worship in January 1865; a few months later the Greyfriars harmonium was replaced by a pipe organ. (See letter of 7th April 1905 from Marshall Lang quoted by John Kerr in *The Renascence of Worship* (1905), p. 90. Fleming, op. cit., p. 120, confusing the Greyfriars harmonium with its pipe organ, back-dates the Anderston organ to 1863 when the church was not in existence; Maxwell, p. 167, unaccountably shifts both organs still further back to 1860.) After 1865 the new instrument multiplied rapidly. In 1868 Boyd could write (p. 172): "In eight churches under the jurisdiction of the Presbytery of Glasgow organs are either in use or in process of erection." R. H. Story got an organ installed in Rosneath in 1873, preceded by a harmonium a few years before (*Memoir* by his daughters, p. 60).

The non-established churches were a little more conservative than the Church of Scotland. In 1856 an organ was installed in Claremont United Presbyterian Church, Glasgow, and the congregation petitioned the Synod (the supreme court of that Church) to sanction its use; the Synod in 1858 refused such sanction, and the ban was not lifted until 1872 (Fleming, op. cit., pp. 117-18). The

Free Church General Assembly in 1858 considered overtures from three Presbyteries (including that of Edinburgh) praying "that in this Church's intercourse with other Churches, regard should be had to purity and uniformity of worship in them". (The allusion was to the Presbyterian Church of England, whose Synod in 1857, while refusing to give any general permission to the use of organs, had tolerated the continuance of the existing instruments at St. John's, Warrington, and St. George's, Liverpool.) There was a full discussion, in the course of which it appeared that the overwhelming majority of the Assembly would wish to abandon mutual eligibility of ministers if the Presbyterian Church of England were to grant a general permission for the use of organs, and the Deliverance passed by the Assembly gave effect to this desire. Votes were not counted but eight members recorded their dissents. (*Free Church Assembly Proceedings*, 1858, pp. 213-21; Fleming, op. cit., pp. 118-19.) The threat to abandon mutual eligibility of ministers never materialized, because by the time organs became general in England the Free Church was no longer so strongly opposed to the "kist o' whistles". Organs were permitted by the Assembly of the Free Church in 1883.

42. Boyd, p. 204; Lee, pp. 29, 79-80; Leishman, p. 405. One would gather from Boyd and Lee that reading of sermons was now universal; indeed in his *Graver Thoughts of a Country Parson* (1862), p. 9, Boyd went so far as to say that "even in Scotland, the fashion of repeating sermons from memory is all but extinct". But these reformers were not above some wishful thinking. A more judicial statement is given in Philp: "It was formerly the universal custom . . . for these discourses to be delivered, like the prayers, extempore; but in large towns, at the present day, many of the ministers read them" (*The Denominational Reason Why*, p. 211). This is condensed from the fuller account given by Jamieson, who explains that reading of sermons began with a few leading Moderates in the eighteenth century, and subsequently became general among clergy of that outlook. In the nineteenth century, however, the practice was adopted also by some leading Evangelicals, e.g. Sir Henry Moncrieff and Dr. Andrew Thomson in Edinburgh and Dr. Thomas Chalmers in Glasgow, and thus by the time of writing (1853) the practice had become quite general in the larger towns, though not in the country. Dr. Norman Macleod preached "entirely extempore" to Queen Victoria at Balmoral on 29th October 1854, as she records in her *Leaves from the Journal of our Life in the Highlands*. See also *Memoirs of James Begg*, by T. Smith (1882), vol. i, pp. 23, 84, and ii,

pp. 326-28, 351-52. Reading of sermons was certainly becoming general in 1860, particularly in the case of younger men, but there was much prejudice to be overcome, especially in country parishes.

43. The Relief Church published its first hymn-book in 1794, the U.P. Church in 1851, the Church of Scotland in 1861, the Free Church in 1873. (McCrie, pp. 332-34; Wright, p. 261; Farmer, pp. 377-78; Maxwell, p. 169. The date 1882 given by Maxwell is the date of the *second* Free Church hymn-book.)

44. Boyd, pp. 183-84; see also Lord Sands, p. 18.

45. Kilmarkie will soon, however, be transferring the second service to the evening. The change took place in the bigger towns in the eighteen-sixties and radiated to the smaller towns. See also note 37. In Rosneath R. H. Story introduced an evening service as early as 1862 (*Memoir*, p. 59). The extent to which evening services had been introduced in England can be seen from the 1851 Census of Religion.

46. Hence the story of the man who on Communion Thursday took occasion to visit a friend in a neighbouring parish, and when his dog strayed asked his friend "Wull ye no' whustle on ma dug? It's Fast Day in oor toon." In more conservative parishes there would be sermons on Fast Day: Jamieson, p. 104.

47. According to Jamieson (p. 106), tent-meetings, though discontinued by 1853 in the south, were retained "in those parishes which lie in the *embouchure* of the Highlands".

48. It was on such an occasion that Dr. Veitch of St. Cuthbert's, Edinburgh, called out to the jostling crowd in the narrow passage "Push not with horn, shove not with the shoulder" (alluding, of course, to Ezekiel 34: 21).

49. According to the Oxford English Dictionary the word purlicue (also spelt perlicue, pirlicue, or even pirlekeu), probably derived from the French *queue*, perhaps from *pour le queue*, came into use in Scotland in the early nineteenth century in the sense of "tailpiece", e.g. a flourish made by a writer at the end of a line. Later it came to be used of the concluding address on the Communion Saturday or Monday, but not long before that address's disappearance.

50. See note 40.

51. "The long tables were never favoured by the Free Church" (Burnet, p. 270). The practice of sitting in the pews to receive the Sacrament (known in the nineteenth century as "simultaneous communion" before Congregationalists developed really simul-

taneous communion by drinking out of separate glasses already placed in the pews) was presumably copied by the Free Church leaders from that of the English Presbyterians, or possibly from the Scottish Independents. The English Dissenters of the seventeenth and eighteenth centuries had retained what had been common usage in the Church of England in the early seventeenth century before Laud instituted a railed-off altar at the east end and insisted that the communicants should take the Sacrament kneeling there. Reception in the pews had the advantage of greatly reducing the time taken in administration. It began to be introduced in the Church of Scotland in the eighteen-twenties, but was condemned by the Assembly of 1825; no doubt the Free Church felt it could disregard this prohibition. (For the change in the Church of Scotland see Sprott, pp. 132-34; Leishman, pp. 421-22; Burnet, pp. 269-71.)

52. Burns, p. 515.

53. For this exception see Boyd, p. 188; for the general practice see Leishman, p. 408; Wright, pp. 160-62; Burns, p. 482; Edgar (II), p. 209. Practice of course varied from one part of the country to another. Jamieson (p. 102a) said in 1853 that "baptism is, for the most part, administered publicly, and, as no objection is made to private baptisms in cases of sickness, inclement weather, or great distance, yet there is a strong feeling in favour of the ordinance being dispensed in the church." Most writers, however, say that in the latter half of the nineteenth century over the country as a whole private baptisms considerably outnumbered public. Queen Victoria, in *More Leaves from a Journal* . . . gave a detailed description of the private baptism of a forester's child on 24th October 1868, and another on 1st November.

54. For the history of marriage ceremonies see Sprott, pp. 146-150; Wright, pp. 151-58; Leishman, p. 413; Edgar (II), pp. 173-74.

55. McMillan, p. 291, and compare the account by Thomas Morer in 1715, reproduced on p. lxix of the Spalding Club's *Selections from Ecclesiastical Records of Aberdeen* (1846).

56. The version given in the Wodrow Society's *Miscellany*, vol. I, pp. 293-300, along with an address and prayer, suggests that this hymn may have continued in use in some places for many years afterwards. Cf. McCrie, pp. 130-32, 291-300.

57. The prohibition in the Book of Discipline (1561) was not quite absolute—see McMillan, pp. 283-86; but even McMillan produces no evidence of any actual worship in connection with burials, apart from funeral sermons.

58. Compare the description of the funeral sermon for the Earl of Leven in 1664 given in Robert Chambers's *Domestic Annals of Scotland* (1858), vol. ii, p. 299.

59. Useful evidence of the date of this change is available from chapter XXXI of Scott's *Antiquary*. After describing the coffining of the fisherman Mucklebackit's son immediately before the procession to the churchyard, Scott comments as follows:

> With a spirit of contradiction, which we may be pardoned for esteeming narrow-minded, the fathers of the Scottish kirk rejected, even on this most solemn occasion, the form of an address to the Divinity, lest they should be thought to give countenance to the rituals of Rome or of England. With much better and more liberal judgment, it is the present practice of most Scottish clergymen to seize this opportunity of offering a prayer, and exhortation, suitable to make an impression upon the living, while they are yet in the very presence of the relics of him, whom they have but lately seen such as they themselves, and who now is such as they must in their time become. But this decent and praiseworthy practice was not adopted at the time of which I am treating, or, at least, Mr Blattergowl [the parish minister] did not act upon it, and the ceremony proceeded without any devotional exercise.

The Antiquary was written in 1816; the events described in it are supposed to have taken place in the last decade of the eighteenth century.

60. *Peter's Letters to his Kinsfolk*, third edition (1819), vol. III, p. 317.

I have received help from many friends in my explorations into the history of Scottish worship, but I wish to acknowledge with special gratitude the help given to me in the preparation of the original booklet by the Rev. Andrew L. Drummond, then of Alva, Clackmannanshire, and by the Rev. Ian A. Muirhead, of the University of Glasgow, in its revision.